Stopwatch

Teacher's Guide

6

Ivor Williams

Richmond

Richmond

58 St Aldates
Oxford
OX1 1ST
United Kingdom

Stopwatch Teacher's Guide Level 6

First Edition: September 2016
Fourth Reprint: July 2019
ISBN: 978-607-06-1246-6

© Text: Ivor Williams
© Richmond Publishing, S.A. de C.V. 2016
Av. Río Mixcoac No. 274, Col. Acacias,
Benito Juárez, C.P. 03240, Ciudad de México

Publisher: Justine Piekarowicz
Editorial Team: Adrián Pliego
Design Team: Jaime Angeles, Daniel Mejía
Pre-Press Coordinator: Daniel Santillán
Pre-Press Team: Susana Alcántara, Virginia Arroyo, Daniel Santillán
Cover Design: Karla Avila
Cover Photograph: © **Shutterstock**

All rights reserved. No part of this work may be reproduced, stored in a retrieval system or transmitted in any form or by any means without prior written permission from the Publisher.

Richmond publications may contain links to third party websites or apps. We have no control over the content of these websites or apps, which may change frequently, and we are not responsible for the content or the way it may be used with our materials. Teachers and students are advised to exercise discretion when accessing the links.

The Publisher has made every effort to trace the owner of copyright material; however, the Publisher will correct any involuntary omission at the earliest opportunity.

Printed in China

Contents

- 4 Scope and Sequence
- 6 Introduction to the Teacher's Guide
- 10 Unit 0 How do you balance work and fun?
- 15 Unit 1 What are you like?
- 29 Unit 2 What could I make?
- 43 Unit 3 How am I different now?
- 57 Unit 4 How green do you want to be?
- 71 Unit 5 Is reality stranger than fiction?
- 85 Unit 6 What would the world be like if…?
- 99 Unit 7 What do I need to live abroad?
- 113 Unit 8 What will I do in the future?
- 126 CD1 and CD2 Contents
- 127 Verb List

Scope and Sequence

Unit	Vocabulary	Grammar	Skills
0 How do you balance work and fun?	**Review:** air travel, food, household chores, life experiences, music, unusual jobs	Present perfect; Phrasal verbs; Second conditional; Passive voice; Defining and non-defining relative clauses	**Listening:** Listening for specific information
1 What are you like?	**Personality Traits:** considerate, dishonest, friendly, honest, impatient, inconsiderate, irresponsible, patient, reasonable, responsible, unfriendly, unreasonable	Tag questions	**Reading:** Understanding implicit information **Speaking:** Role-playing a job interview **Project:** Creating a personality quiz
2 What could I make?	**Materials and Tools:** drill, glue stick, hammer, hot glue gun, nails, plywood, saw, screwdriver, screws, solder, soldering iron	Passive voice (present simple, present continuous, past simple, future, present perfect, modals)	**Listening:** Identifying steps in instructions **Writing:** Writing instructions **Project:** Presenting a life hack
3 How am I different now?	**Milestones:** attend acting classes, build a drone, create a vlog, develop a computer game, get a part-time job, learn another language, start a band with friends, write a book	Present perfect vs. present perfect continuous	**Reading:** Predicting content **Speaking:** Talking about a life-changing experience **Project:** Creating a vlog
4 How green do you want to be?	**Sustainable Living:** baking soda, carpool, food leftovers, indoor garden, rechargeable batteries, reusable shopping bags, vinegar	First conditional vs. second conditional	**Listening:** Identifying opinions and facts **Writing:** Writing a report **Project:** Creating an action plan to implement a green initiative at school

Unit	Vocabulary	Grammar	Skills
5 Is reality stranger than fiction?	**Strange Creatures and Phenomena:** aliens, clairvoyance, ghosts, telekinesis, telepathy, UFOs, werewolves, zombies	Perfect modals	**Reading:** Reading for main ideas **Writing:** Writing an explanation based on graphic organizers **Project:** Making a presentation about an unsolved mystery
6 What would the world be like if…?	**Milestones of the 21st Century:** achieve a breakthrough, break out, disaster, fight a war, go through a crisis, hit, lead a revolution, make a discovery, pandemic	Third conditional; Mixed conditional	**Listening:** Distinguishing facts from opinions **Speaking:** Discussing a historical issue **Project:** Writing a homepage of an online newspaper
7 What do I need to live abroad?	**Living Abroad:** apply for a student visa, buy plane tickets, choose a language school, enroll in a course, fill out forms, get a passport, make new friends, make travel arrangements, participate in cultural events, take out travel insurance, try local foods	Reported statements	**Reading:** Reading for specific details **Writing:** Writing a leaflet **Project:** Preparing a section of a guide for foreign college students
8 What will I do in the future?	**Future Goals:** be more sympathetic to others, buy a car, buy a house, get married, get a job after college, go to college, have a healthier lifestyle, rent an apartment, save money, start a business, travel the world	Future continuous	**Listening:** Inferring information **Speaking:** Giving a presentation **Project:** Writing an action plan for the future

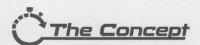
The Concept

Stopwatch is a motivating, six-level secondary series built around the concept of visual literacy.

- *Stopwatch* constructs students' language skills from A0 to B1 of the Common European Framework of Reference (CEFR).
- A stopwatch symbolizes energy, speed, movement and competition and gives immediate feedback. The *Stopwatch* series offers dynamic, engaging activities and timed challenges that encourage students to focus and train for mastery.
- *Stopwatch* has a strong visual component to facilitate and deepen learning through authentic tasks, compelling images and the use of icons.
- The series was conceived for the international market, with a wide range of topics, incorporating cultures from around the world.

- The six-level framework of the series allows for different entry points to fit the needs of each school or group of students.
- The syllabus has been carefully structured. Each level recycles and expands on the language that was used in the previous books. This process of spiraled language development helps students internalize what they are learning.
- Each level of *Stopwatch* covers 90 – 120 hours of classroom instruction, plus an additional 20 hours of supplementary activities and materials in the Teacher's Guide and Teacher's Toolkit.

The Components

Student's Book & Workbook

Units are divided into distinct spreads, each with a clear focus:

- A **Big Question** establishes the central theme of the unit and promotes critical thinking, curiosity and interest in learning.
- **Vocabulary** is presented in thematic sets and with rich visual support to convey meaning.
- **Grammar** is introduced in context, enabling students to see the meaning, form and use of the structure.
- **Skills** (reading, listening, writing and speaking) are developed through engaging topics.
- **Culture** invites the learner to immerse oneself in the rich variety of cultures and peoples on our planet.

- **Review** activities provide consolidated practice for each of the grammar and vocabulary areas.
- In the **Project**, students apply the skills they learned in the unit to a creative task built around the Big Question.
- **Just for Fun** is a page with fun activities that teachers can assign to fast finishers.
- The **Workbook** pages offer extended practice with the vocabulary, structures and skills of the unit.
- The **Student's CD** contains all the listening material in the units.

Teacher's Guide

Brief instructions or summaries provide a quick guide for each Student's Book activity, including **answer keys** and **audio scripts**.

A fun and engaging **warm-up** activity reviews previous knowledge and prepares students for what will be seen in each lesson.

A **wrap-up** task practices newly-learned material. Warm-ups and wrap-ups usually take the form of games.

Extension tasks promote use of language in communication and real-life situations.

Digital options provide alternatives to the projects using electronic media.

Specific questions, related to the Big Question of the unit, stimulate critical thinking.

Teaching tips help develop and enrich teachers' skills.

Teacher's Toolkit (printable materials)

The Teacher's Toolkit is a comprehensive resource that is delivered in two CDs.

🔴 **CD1** includes the Class Audio and Worksheets

Worksheets
- Grammar Worksheets (2 per unit) with Answer Key
- Reading Worksheets (2 per unit) with Guidelines and Answer Key
- Vocabulary Worksheets (2 per unit) with Answer Key

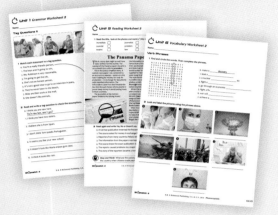

🔴 **CD2** includes Project Rubrics, Score Cards, Tests and Test Audios

Project Rubrics
- These contain proposed criteria that can be used to evaluate students' performance in the completion of the unit projects.

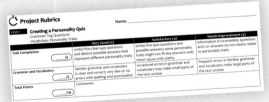

Scorecard
- These help students evaluate their progress by reflecting on their newly-acquired grammar, vocabulary, reading and listening skills.

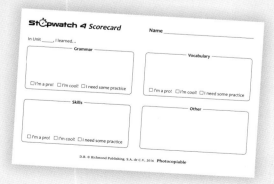

Tests

- **Placement Tests** (Beginner & Intermediate) with Grading Scale and Answer Key

These will help teachers assess students' level of English on an individual and group basis and select appropriate tests.

- **Standard Tests** (1 per unit) with Answer Key

These cover the vocabulary and grammar from the units, as well as reading and listening skills.

- **Tests Plus** (1 per unit) with Answer Key

These are the **extended** version of the Standard Tests, which include an additional communication component designed to assess speaking and writing.

- **Mid-Term Tests** with Answer Key

These should be given out after having completed U4.

- **Final Tests** with Answer Key

These should be given out after having completed U8.

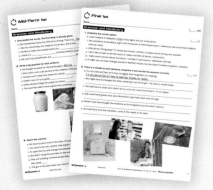

The Big Question: What are you like?

- **Student's Book & Workbook**

Unit Opener

Visual prompts establish context and promote discussion

Vertical orientation of some sections to conform to visual requirements

Timed game-like activity

Vocabulary

Insight to language or content

Grammar

Audios available on CD and in the Digital Book

Visual literacy development

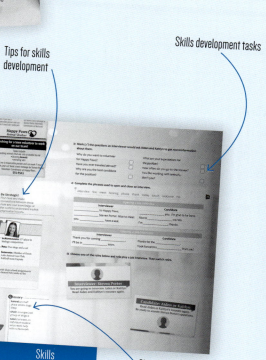

Skills

Two skills per unit

Tips for skills development

Skills development tasks

Critical thinking tasks

Glossary of new words

• Student's Book & Workbook

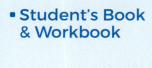

Content relevant to students' lives

Level-appropriate language encourages learner engagement

Critical thinking / Value tasks

Culture

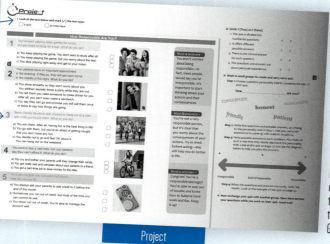

Linguistic and conceptual preparation for the project

Sample of the project

Digital options for the project in the Teacher's Guide

Project

Activities for fast finishers

Just for Fun

Topics expand on the unit theme

Review

More practice with unit grammar and vocabulary

Workbook section

How do you balance work and fun?

Grammar	Vocabulary
Present Perfect: <u>Have</u> you ever <u>gone</u> camping? **Modal Verbs:** might, could, may, can't **Past Perfect:** When I arrived at the party, Emma <u>had</u> already <u>left</u>. **Second Conditional:** If I <u>didn't have</u> to study, I <u>would go</u> out with my friends. **Passive Voice:** The poultry <u>is fried</u> for 8 minutes or until browned. **Defining and Non-defining Relative Clauses:** Curling, <u>which is an Olympic sport</u>, is practiced on ice.	**Music genres:** classical, country, Latin, pop, reggae, world music **Verb-noun and verb-adverb collocations:** ride a horse, camp overnight, learn to play a musical instrument, perform in a play, travel by plane **Phrasal Verbs:** hang up, pick up, put away, take out, wipe off **Air Travel:** airport, baggage, boarding pass, customs, destination, flight, luggage, passport, plane

10

Reading	Listening
Reading for specific information	Listening to check information

In the first lesson, read the unit title aloud and have students look carefully at the unit cover. Encourage them to think about the message in the picture. At the end of the unit, students will discuss the big question: *How do you balance work and fun?*

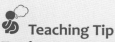 **Teaching Tip**
Teacher Expectations
Start the new course by making clear what you expect from students. You may choose to mention some or all of the following:
You expect students to make an effort to participate in class.
You expect them to 'have a go' and to not worry about making mistakes, which – you should remind them – are an essential part of learning.
You expect students to work on their own outside class. Also, remind students that it is perfectly okay for them to ask you for help if they need it.

Lesson 1 Student's Book p. 8

Warm-up
Students recap what they studied in their previous English course.
- Organize students into small groups and have them brainstorm topics, skills, grammar, vocabulary, etc. that they studied in their previous English course. Invite students to talk about the activities in English class that they most enjoy.

1 Read the song titles and their artists on the playlist. Match each of them with its genre.
Students match song titles with genres of popular music.
- Ask students to look at the list. Elicit that it is someone's personal playlist of favorite songs. Elicit or point out that the pieces are from a variety of different musical genres. Have students read the titles and match each one with the correct genre. Check answers.

Answers
1. reggae, 2. classical, 3. world music, 4. Latin, 5. pop, 6. country

- Draw students' attention to the *Guess What!* box. Read the information aloud and elicit observation and comment. Ask students if they are familiar with the song "See You Again".

2 Think Fast! In your notebook, write song titles for these music genres: *country, pop, rap, reggae, rock* and *world music*.
Students do a 30-second timed challenge: writing song titles (real or made up) for various genres of music
- Set the time limit and have students work in pairs coming up with song titles for each of the musical genres. Check and discuss answers.

Answers
Answers will vary.

3 Match the verbs to the phrases. Then number the pictures the activities refer to. Two pictures will not be used.
Students match verbs with noun phrases and adverb phrases to form collocations.
- Ask students to look at the first item. Elicit a word of phrase from the column on the right that collocates well with this verb (*overnight*), then have students work alone or in pairs completing the rest of the activity. Check answers.

Answers
1. overnight, 2. your look, 3. your own web page, 4. to play a musical instrument, 5. in a play, 6. a horse, 7. a boat, 8. by plane
top to bottom, first column 2, 1 *top to bottom, second column* 8, 5 *top to bottom, third column* [these two pictures are not used] *top to bottom, fourth column* 4, 3, 7, 6

> ### Extension
> Students prepare presentations about traditional folk music in their country.
> - Organize students into small groups and have them look for information about traditional types of folk music in their country. Invite them to give presentations, including samples of music (live or recorded), for the rest of the class.

Wrap-up
Students compile music playlists for their classmates.
- Organize students into pairs and have each student first work alone compiling a playlist for their partner. Then ask students to exchange playlists and to say whether their partner chose music that they like.

 (No homework today.)

> ### Teaching Tip
> **Keeping Vocabulary Notes**
> Suggest to students that they keep separate vocabulary notes. These can be kept on sheets in a folder and organized according to lexical sets. Encourage students to add new words and phrases in the appropriate existing section, and to create new sections, as they progress through the course.

Lesson 2   Student's Book p. 9

Warm-up

Students share information about things that they have done.

- Organize students into small groups. Ask them to each write three present perfect sentences – one of them true and two of them false – about things they have done in their life and to share them with the people in their group. Their classmates try to decide which is the true statement.

4 Complete the questions in the quiz. Then answer them.
Students complete present perfect questions and then answer them.

- Ask students to look at the text. Elicit that it is a quiz to determine how interested the reader is in trying new things. First, have students work alone completing the questions in the quiz. Then ask students to answer the questions honestly.

Answers
1. *Have you ever gone camping?* 2. Have you ever changed your look? 3. Have you ever designed a web page? 4. Have you ever learned to play a musical instrument? 5. Have you ever performed in a play? 6. Have you ever ridden a horse? 7. Have you ever sailed a boat?

5 Work with a partner. Share your answers in Activity 4. Ask for further information.
Students share and compare their answers to a quiz.

- Organize students into pairs and ask them to share and compare their answers to the quiz in the previous activity and to offer additional information. Then discuss their answers as a whole class.

Answers
Answers will vary.

Stop and Think! Critical Thinking
Which of the activities in Activity 3 would you **never** like to do for fun? Why?

- Organize students into small groups and have them discuss which of the activities in Activity 3 they would never like to do for fun. Encourage them to give their reasons.
- Invite groups to share their comments with the rest of the class.

6 🎧¹ Rewrite the numbered sentences, replacing the phrases in italics with the corresponding phrasal verb. Then listen and check your answers.
Students rewrite sentences using phrasal verbs.

- Ask students to read through the whole conversation. Then ask them to look at the first item and have them say which phrasal verb can replace the verb (*pick up*). Then have students work alone or in pairs completing the rest of the exercise. Then have students listen to check their answers.

Answers
1. I have picked up my socks. 2. I have hung up my clothes. 3. And have you wiped off your desk? 4. Have you put them away? 5. Now could you take out the garbage?

Audio Script
DAD: Have you cleaned your room?
SARAH: Yes, I have, Dad. I have picked up my socks and I have hung up my clothes.
DAD: Good! And have you wiped off your desk? It was very dusty.
SARAH: Yes, Dad. And I have washed the cloth I used.
DAD: What about the books under your bed? Have you put them away?
SARAH: Of course, Dad. They're on the bookshelf.
DAD: That's great, Sarah. Now could you take out the garbage, please?
SARAH: But, Dad…
DAD: I don't want to hear any complaints, young lady! Your room was a mess, and you know that everybody needs to help around the house!

Wrap-up
Students role-play conversations like the one in Activity 6.

- Organize students into pairs and invite them to role-play conversations in which a parent asks their teenage son or daughter about the chores they have done. Have pairs of students share their work with the rest of the class.

(No homework today.)

Lesson 3 Student's Book p. 10

Warm-up
Students recap past simple, present perfect and past perfect.
- Briefly review these tenses by reading out a random selection of sentences in the past simple, the present perfect or the past perfect, and asking students to identify the tense in each case.

7 Read the sentences. What happened first? Number 1 and 2.
Students read past perfect sentences and say which of two actions occurred first.
- Read aloud the first item and ask students to say which action happened first (*Emma left the party.*), then have students work alone or in pairs completing the rest of the exercise. Check answers and deal with any queries about the past perfect that students may have.

Answers
1. (1) Emma left the party. (2) I arrived at the party. 2. (1) Alexis cleaned her room. (2) Alexis went out with her friends. 3. (1) Ethan and Dave finished the test. (2) The class finished. 4. (1) Andrew went home. (2) I got to the mall to meet Andrew.

8 Read the situations below. Write second conditional sentences.
Students write second conditional sentences from prompts.
- Ask students to look at the first pair of sentences and at the second conditional sentence that combines the two ideas. Ask students to work alone or in pairs, writing second conditional sentences from the cues. Check answers and deal with any queries about the second conditional that students may have.

Answers
1. *If I didn't have to study, I would go out with my friends.* 2. Kylie would go to the movies if she had some money. 3. If Ann and Jim weren't too young to get a job, they would work. 4. We'd love to walk to school if it wasn't so far from home. 5. If I spoke German, I could talk to my cousin in Munich.

9 Complete the diagram with the words in the box.
Students complete a diagram with vocabulary related to air travel.
- Ask students to look at the activity. Elicit that all of the sentences are to do with air travel. Ask students to look at the first item. Elicit the correct answer (*flight*), then have students work alone or in pairs completing the rest of the exercise. Check answers.

Answers
1. flight, 2. airport, 3. boarding pass, 4. luggage, 5. passport, 6. plane, [7.], 8. destination, 9. customs, 10. baggage

Wrap-up
Students create vocabulary diagrams like the one in Activity 9.
- Organize students into pairs and have them create diagrams like the one in Activity 9 but about other topics and other processes, for example, the first day of school, going to a concert, etc.
- Have students display their work around the classroom.

 (No homework today.)

> ### Teaching Tip
> **Using Non-verbal Cues**
> Remember to use visuals, sketches, gestures, intonation, and other non-verbal cues to make both your language and the content of the lesson more accessible to your students.

Unit 0

Lesson 4   Student's Book p. 11

Warm-up

Students recap first, second and third conditionals.
- Briefly review conditional sentences by writing on the board a series of conditional sentences and asking students to identify each one.

10 Complete the sentences with your own ideas. Use *might*, *could*, *may* or *can't*, depending on how possible the sentences are.

Students write sentences using modal verbs to express degrees of possibility.
- Read aloud the first sentence opening and orally elicit ideas for ways to complete it using a modal from the list. Then have students work alone completing the sentences with their own ideas. Check and discuss answers.

Answers

Answers will vary.

11 Read the extracts of cooking directions. Do the tasks below. Match the extracts to the dishes. Underline the verbs for cooking methods. Mark (✓) the extracts in the passive voice.

Students read cooking instructions and carry out a series of tasks.
- Ask students to read the texts and to match each one with the correct photo. Then have them underline the verbs that relate to cooking processes. Finally, ask students to identify which of the four texts use the passive voice.

Answers

match 1. Chicken Kebabs and Vegetable Couscous, 2. Spicy Turkey with Green Beans, 3. Crunchy Chocolate Chip Cookies, 4. Homemade Charcoal Burger *verbs for cooking methods* roast, boil, fried, browned, bake, grilled *extracts in the passive voice* 2, 4

12 In your notebook, rewrite the statements in the passive voice.

Students rewrite active voice sentences in the passive voice.
- Ask students to look at all four sentences. Elicit or point out that they are in different tenses. (You may wish to ask students to identify them.) Ask students to convert each sentence into the passive voice. Check answers and deal with any questions that students may have about the passive voice.

Answers

1. Too much fat is consumed (by people) in this country. 2. Vacation days for employees have been reduced (by companies). 3. The bedrooms and the kitchen were cleaned (by them) yesterday. 4. Kebabs with chicken, beef and vegetables are being made (by the cooks).

13 Circle the correct option. Then decide if the sentences are defining (*D*) or non-defining (*ND*) relative clauses.

Students identify the correct relative pronoun in a series of sentences.
- Ask students to look at the four items. Elicit or point out that they all contain relative clauses. Ask students first to circle the correct relative pronoun in each pair of options, then have them mark the sentences *D* for defining relative clause or *ND* for non-defining relative clause. Check answers and deal with any queries that students may have regarding relative clauses and relative pronouns.

Answers

1. that D, 2. who ND, 3. which ND, 4. that D

Big Question

Students are given the opportunity to revisit the Big Question and reflect on it.
- Ask students to turn to the unit opener on page 7 and look again at the collage of photos. Elicit observation and comment about the images – the ones that represent work and the ones that represent fun.
- Read aloud the question. Discuss how some people – both students and adults – can sometimes find it hard to achieve a balance between obligations related to work and the need for fun and relaxation.

➡ **(No homework today.)**

What are you like?

Grammar	Vocabulary
Tag questions: He has a lot of pets, <u>doesn't he</u>?	**Personality traits:** considerate, friendly, honest, patient, reasonable, responsible **Adjective prefixes:** <u>im</u>patient, <u>in</u>considerate, <u>un</u>friendly

Reading	Speaking
Activating existing knowledge Reading for specific information	Role-playing a job interview

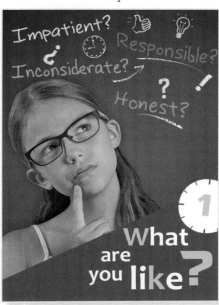

In the first lesson, read the unit title aloud and have students look carefully at the unit cover. Encourage them to think about the message in the picture. At the end of the unit, students will discuss the big question: *What are you like?*

Teaching Tip
Keeping a Grammar Notebook
Encourage students to keep a notebook for all the grammar that they study during this level of the course. Notebook entries could include tables, explanations, diagrams, timelines, etc. with students' own sample sentences that illustrate the target structure.

 **Vocabulary**

Objective
Students will be able to use **personality traits** and **adjectives prefixes** vocabulary to talk about what people are like.

Lesson 1 Student's Book p. 14

Warm-up

Students complete sentences about themselves using personality adjectives.

- Brainstorm with the class four or five superheroes (like Spiderman, Batman, etc.).
- Write the superheroes' names on the board and ask students to list adjectives that could describe what the hero is like on the board under each name, for example, *brave, strong, smart,* etc.
- Then write on the board *I think I am… My friends think I am… My [family member] thinks I am…* and tell students to complete the sentences about themselves using the adjectives on the board. For the third sentence, students fill in a family relationship (*mom, brother, grandpa,* etc.).
- Have students share their sentences in small groups.

1 Read the leaflet and circle two words that describe personality traits.

Students practice personality traits vocabulary by identifying vocabulary words in a text.

Answers

responsible, honest

2 Match the sentence halves to create definitions of people's traits.

Students combine sentence halves to make definitions of personality traits.

Answers

top to bottom 5, 1, 6, 4, 3, 2

3 Think Fast! Name the positive forms of *irresponsible, dishonest* and *unfriendly*, as fast as you can!

Students do a thirty-second timed challenge: they name the antonyms of the adjectives with prefixes.

- Draw students' attention to the *Guess What!* box. Read the information aloud and discuss the adjective prefixes. Elicit other prefixes (*dis-, il-, ir-*) that students may know.

Answers

responsible, honest, friendly

Wrap-up

Students invent funny nicknames for fictional characters.

- Invite students to invent nicknames for people, using an adjective that begins with the same letter as the person's name, for example, *Friendly Fernanda, Reasonable Richard,* etc. Students can draw simple cartoons of their characters, showing that particular personality trait.

 Workbook p. 126, Activities 1 and 2

> **Teaching Tip**
> **Having Fun With Language**
> Encourage students to play with language and to share their enjoyment of words that they think sound funny, of tongue twisters, of bizarre names of places, etc.

Lesson 2 — Student's Book p. 15

✔ **Homework Check!**
Workbook p. 126, Activities 1 and 2

Answers

1 Find six positive personality traits in the word search.

```
F B I X D C A Y V N Z X X
R H E T A R E D I S N O C
I I R Y P P W T Z E V T P
E H B G V Y I H Q W D B A
N S X F B L G O E L C P T
D H R E A S O N A B L E I
L J M R T A S E U H R E E
F Z X S L O S Z I J S N
I Q A D G J C T O W Z X T
G F E L B I S N O P S E R
```

1. considerate, 2. patient, 3. honest, 4. reasonable, 5. responsible

2 Complete the chart with the negative forms of the adjectives in Activity 1.
im-, ir-, in- inconsiderate, irresponsible,
un- unfriendly, unreasonable, *dis-* dishonest

Warm-up
Students practice personality adjectives by performing skits.
- Divide students into small groups of three or four and write the personality adjectives on separate slips of paper, with one adjective for each group.
- One student from each group chooses a slip of paper. The group develops a brief skit to illustrate their personality adjective. They must not say the adjective or any form of the adjective in their skit.
- Groups perform their skits for the class and other groups try to guess the adjective each skit is illustrating. Groups get one point for each correct guess and one point if others correctly guess their adjective.

4 Look at the pictures and complete the sentences.
Students complete descriptions with the most appropriate personality adjectives.

Answers
1. dishonest, 2. considerate, 3. patient,
4. reasonable, 5. unfriendly, 6. irresponsible

5 Discuss what personality traits you think Bea and Mike have.
Students look at photos and speculate about people's personalities.

6 Listen and check your predictions.
Students listen and confirm their predictions about Bea ad Mike.

Audio Script
BEA: So, Mike... check out this ad looking for a fundraising volunteer! Have you seen it?
MIKE: No... Who posted it?
BEA: Happy Paws! I know how much you love animals, so I thought you'd be interested in it!
MIKE: Yes, I love animals! But I'm not sure I'm the right person for *this* position...
BEA: Why not? You're so responsible! And definitely the most honest guy I know...
MIKE: Yeah... but, you know, this volunteer needs to be nice and friendly, talk to store owners to convince them to get a collection can... I'm too impatient for that.
BEA: Well, you're right about *that*!
MIKE: Why don't *you* apply to it?
BEA: Me?
MIKE: Of course! You're so considerate and reasonable, you'll be able to convince store owners easily! Besides, your friendly attitude is perfect for the job!
BEA: Hmm... I guess I'll think about it!
MIKE: You really should!

7 Listen again and write what Bea and Mike say, according to how they describe themselves and each other.
Students listen again and take notes about what Bea and Mike say they are like.

Answers
Bea considerate, reasonable, friendly
Mike responsible, honest, impatient

Stop and Think! Critical Thinking
What personality traits should volunteers working in different areas have? Why?
- Brainstorm some areas that people volunteer in as a class (healthcare, cleaning up a city, tutoring younger children, etc.).
- Organize students into small groups and have them discuss the traits that volunteers in each area should have. (If necessary, write ideas on the board to get them started.)
- Invite groups to share their comments with the rest of the class.

Wrap-up
Students describe imagined friends and family for Bea and Mike.
- In small groups, tell students to imagine what, for example, Mike's parents are like and to describe them using personality adjectives.

➡ **Workbook pp. 126 and 127, Activities 3 and 4**

Grammar

Objective
Students will be able to use **tag questions** to confirm information.

Lesson 3 — Student's Book p. 16

> ✔ **Homework Check!**
> Workbook pp. 126 and 127, Activities 3 and 4
> **Answers**
> **3 Complete each sentence with a word in the box.**
> 1. honest, 2. irresponsible, 3. patient,
> 4. unreasonable, 5. friendly
> **4 Circle the correct word to complete the quotes.**
> 1. responsible, 2. patience, 3. unfriendly,
> 4. Perseverance

Warm-up
Students play a game to review personality traits vocabulary.
- Students form pairs. Tell them to look at the dogs and cats in the photos on pages 16 and 17 and write down two or three personality adjectives to describe each animal.
- Pairs take turns with another pair describing the animals' personalities to each other and see if they can guess which animal the other pair is describing.

1 Look at the picture and the words below. Make predictions about what is happening.
Students use vocabulary and a visual prompt to make predictions about a situation.

2 🎧³ Listen and check your predictions. Then choose the correct option to complete the sentences.
Students listen to confirm answers and complete summarizing sentences.

Answers
1. at Happy Paws' office. 2. an interviewer and a candidate for a volunteer position.

Audio Script
STEVEN: Hi, welcome to our office, Bea. Please sit down.
BEA: Thanks. I'm glad to be here.
STEVEN: This is not your first time at Happy Paws, is it?
BEA: No, it isn't. I came here with my friend Mike last week.
STEVEN: I see. Your CV is impressive! I see you did volunteer work at Nursing Care last year, didn't you?
BEA: Yes, I did. It was a great experience.
STEVEN: But you haven't worked there this year, have you?
BEA: No, it was a one-year program, and they closed it this year.
STEVEN: Oh, yes, their volunteer program was excellent, wasn't it? It's a shame they had to close it down.
BEA: Yes, I really enjoyed working there.
STEVEN: And I see from your CV that you don't have any pets. You like pets, don't you?
BEA: Yes, I do! I love animals.
STEVEN: But you don't have any fundraising experience, do you?
BEA: Well… no, I don't. But I'm eager to learn how to do it.
STEVEN: This is great!

3 🎧³ Listen again and match each statement to a tag question.
Students listen again to an interview and match statements with question tags.
- Draw students' attention to the **Tag Questions** box and clarify any doubts students may have.

Answers
1. b, 2. e, 3. f, 4. d, 5. c, 6. a

> **Extension**
> Students discuss volunteer activities.
> - Organize students into groups and invite them to share knowledge and experience of volunteer work. Encourage them to ask each other questions about their experience and to use tag questions.

Wrap-up
Students race to write the correct tag questions on the board.
- Students form teams and line up at the board.
- For each turn, one student from each team comes up to the board to write. Read the beginning of a question for the students at the board to complete with a tag question.
- Some example questions are 1. *She likes animals, … ?*, 2. *He doesn't have any experience, … ?*, 3. *You are available on weekends, … ?*, 4. *I'm not late for the interview, … ?* Answers: 1. doesn't she, 2. does he, 3. aren't you, 4. am I
- The student who writes first the correct tag question on the board wins a point for his or her team.

➡ **Workbook p. 127, Activities 1 and 2**

> 💭 **Teaching Tip**
> **Making Your Own Grammar Practice Exercises**
> At the end of a section of grammar study, invite students to try writing their own practice exercises based on the material on the relevant pages. Students can make copies of their exercises and exchange them with their classmates.

Lesson 4 Student's Book p. 17

✔ **Homework Check!**
Workbook p. 127, Activities 1 and 2
Answers
1 Complete the sentences with a tag in the box.
1. isn't she, 2. did it, 3. didn't they, 4. will he,
5. aren't we
2 Correct the mistakes in the tag questions.
1. didn't it, 2. is it, 3. can't you

Warm-up

Students play Last Man Standing to practice tag questions.
- Prepare questions using tags and find a soft ball or object you can toss to students.
- Have the class stand up. Toss the ball to the first student, and say the beginning of a question for the student to complete with a tag question. If the student says the correct tag question, he or she tosses the ball back to you. If the student doesn't say the correct tag question, he or she tosses the ball back to you and sits down. Repeat with the rest of the class.
- The last students left standing win the game.

4 Complete with tag questions.
Students complete tag questions with the correct endings.
- Draw students' attention to the **Intonation in Tag Questions** box and answer any questions students may have. Ask them to practice saying the tag questions with falling or rising intonation.
- Draw students' attention to the **Guess What!** box. Read the information aloud and discuss how this tag question is an exceptional case.

5 🎧⁴ Listen and check your answers.
Students listen to confirm their answers to Activity 4.
Answers
1. do you? 2. didn't she? 3. won't they? 4. am I?
5. wasn't he? 6. have you? 7. is he? 8. is she?

Audio Script
1. You don't do volunteer work, do you?
2. Bea did well on the interview, didn't she?
3. Happy Paws will hire only one volunteer, won't they?
4. I'm not a very patient person, am I?
5. The interviewer was nice to Bea, wasn't he?
6. You haven't seen the ad on the school board, have you?
7. Mike isn't going to get the position, is he?
8. Bea isn't doing volunteer work at Nursing Care now, is she?

6 🎧⁵ Listen and practice the tag questions.
Students listen for the intonation of tag questions and practice.

Audio Script
You haven't worked at Happy Paws, have you?
Bea is applying for the job, isn't she?
You haven't worked at Happy Paws, have you?
Bea is applying for the job, isn't she?

7 Work with a partner. Take turns practicing the tag questions in Activity 4.
Students work in pairs practicing saying tag questions.

8 Think Fast! Write two other statements followed by tag questions which the interviewer could ask Bea to confirm information from her resume.
Students do a one-minute timed challenge: they write two more tag questions for an interview.

Wrap-up

Students play a guessing game using tag questions.
- Organize students into teams of two or three players. One team chooses an activity or event that they took part in recently. Then, without mentioning the event, they exchange tag questions about it and students from other teams listen and try to guess what the first team is discussing. For example, *We had to wait a long time, didn't we? It was really exciting, wasn't it? You were a little scared, weren't you?* (an amusement park).

➡ **Workbook p. 128, Activity 3**

Reading & Speaking

Objectives
Students will be able to activate existing knowledge and read for specific information. They will also be able to role-play a job interview.

Lesson 5 — Student's Book p. 18

> ✔ **Homework Check!**
> Workbook p. 128, Activity 3
>
> **Answers**
> **3 Complete each sentence with a tag question. Then match the sentences to the pictures.**
> 1. isn't he, 2. wasn't it, 3. isn't she, 4. will he, 5. don't they
> *left to right, top to bottom* 1, 0, 4, 2, 5, 3

Warm-up
Students create short volunteer position advertisements.
- Have students form small groups and tell them to open their books to page 14 and re-read the ad for the volunteer position at Happy Paws.
- Tell students they will create ads for the position. They can use 140 characters or less, including a hashtag to identify their advertisement.
- Encourage groups to first discuss what information from the ad on page 14 is most important to include.
- Groups share their ads with the class.

1 Read the ad for another position at Happy Paws. Circle T (True) or F (False).
Students read an ad and find specific information.
- First, ask students to identify the text type and where it comes from (an ad in a local newspaper).
- Then have students read the ad and the statements carefully and mark each statement true or false.

Answers
1. T, 2. T, 3. F

2 Read the resumes. Write A or K next to the questions below.
Students read teens' resumes and find specific information.
- Draw students' attention to the **Be Strategic!** box and ask them to read the information. Remind students to draw on their existing knowledge of the world to help them understand texts.

Answers
1. A, 2. K, 3. A, 4. K

Stop and Think! Critical Thinking
Why do you think it is important to be a volunteer?
- Organize students into small groups and have them brainstorm ideas about the importance of volunteer work. (If necessary, write some ideas on the board to get them started.)
- Invite groups to share their ideas with the rest of the class.

Extension
Students talk about volunteer work in the place where they live.
- Organize students into small groups and invite them to exchange information about local volunteer projects that they take part in or that they know about.

Wrap-up
Students write their own resumes.
- Invite students to create their own resumes using the ones on page 18 as models. Have them include information that is relevant to the Happy Paws job ad.

 Workbook p. 129, Activities 1 and 2

> **Teaching Tip**
> **Managing Fast Finishers**
> Some students complete activities more quickly than others, so it's a good idea to have a few extra activities on hand, otherwise these students may become bored and disruptive. One set of activities designed for fast finishers is the *Just for Fun* page. Students can work on the activities individually and then check their answers in the back of the Student's Book. The *Just for Fun* activities for this unit are on page 26.

Lesson 6 Student's Book p. 19

> ✔ **Homework Check!**
> Workbook p. 129, Activities 1 and 2
> **Answers**
> **1 Read the text and complete it with the headings of three of the tips.**
> b, a, c
> **2 Read and rank the volunteers from 1 – 3 with 1 having the best chance to get the volunteer position at Happy Paws.**
> *top to bottom* 2, 1, 3

Warm-up

Students play a memory game about the candidates from the previous lesson.
- Read aloud a series of statements, some true and some false, about Aiden and Kaitlyn, the candidates from the previous lesson, and have students say which are true and which are false.

3 Mark (✓) the questions an interviewer would ask Aiden and Kaitlyn to get more information about them.
Students select the questions that are relevant to a specific interview.

Answers
left column, top to bottom: 1st, 3rd
right column, top to bottom: 1st, 3rd

4 Complete the phrases used to open and close an interview.
Students complete greetings and leave-taking expressions with the correct words.

Answers
Opening: Interviewer Welcome, I'm, Please, *Candidate* Thank, meet, fine
Closing: Interviewer today, touch, *Candidate* interview, hearing

5 Choose one of the roles below and role-play a job interview. Then switch roles.
Students role-play job interviews for the volunteer position at Happy Paws.

Wrap-up

Students debate which candidate is best for the job.
- Assign students to small groups and tell each group whether they will argue that Aiden or Kaitlyn is the best candidate for the volunteer job.
- Have two groups debate each other at a time, taking turns to share their reasons for preferring Aiden or Kaitlyn.
- After each debate, have the class vote on which side won the argument.

➡ **Workbook p. 129, Activity 3**

Preparing for the Next Lesson
Ask students to watch a video about fetishes made by the Zuni people of New Mexico: http://goo.gl/ClfdBU or invite them to consult official website of the Zuni tribe: http://www.ashiwi.org.

 Culture

Objective
Students will be able to appreciate diversity of cultures and discuss people's attitudes toward animals.

Lesson 7   Student's Book pp. 20 and 21

> ✔ Homework Check!
> Workbook p. 129, Activity 3
> **Answers**
> **3 Work with a partner. Complete a mind map in your notebook with your own ideas about one of the tips below. Then write about the tip.**
> Answers will vary.

 22

Warm-up
Students play a vocabulary game about animals.
- Find a ball or another soft object to toss to students and tell students to stand up.
- Tell students that you will say the name of an animal, and whoever gets the ball has to say either an animal that eats that animal or one that is eaten by it. (Example: *wolf – a wolf eats a rabbit; rabbit – a rabbit is eaten by an owl*, and so on.)
- If the student correctly names another animal in the food chain, he or she tosses the ball to another student. If the student cannot think of another animal in the food chain or is incorrect, he or she tosses the ball to you and sits down.
- Model the activity with a student before beginning. Continue as time allows or until only a few students are left standing.

1 Label the pictures of the animals.
Students label photos of animals with the correct names from the box.

Answers
left to right, top to bottom mountain lion, wolf, bear, coyote, badger, mole, eagle

2 Complete the first column of the chart according to your associations between the animals and the words.
Students complete a chart with their ideas about animals.

Answers
Answers will vary.

3 Read and compare the information with your ideas in Activity 2. Complete the second column of the chart.
Students read the text about Zuni animal fetishes and compare the information with their own ideas.

Answers
1. mole, 2. mountain lion, 3. eagle, 4. bear,
5. badger, 6. wolf, 7. coyote

Wrap-up
Students design their own versions of animal fetishes.
- As a class project, invite students to draw their own designs for a piece of animal fetish artwork. They can use the information in the text or their own ideas about the special characteristics of a certain animal. Have them write short explanatory texts next to their designs.
- Display students' work around the classroom.

▶ **(No homework today.)**

> 💭 **Teaching Tip**
> **Organizing Project Work**
> When giving students any type of project work, make sure that they are very clear about what it is that they have to produce and how much time they have to produce it. A clearly defined end product and a clear timeframe will help to focus students' attention on the task and help them to finish in the time given.

Lesson 8 Student's Book p. 21

Warm-up
Students recap information from the article about the Zuni people.
- In a quick-fire quiz format, test students on what they can remember about the Zuni people and the associations that they make between animals and some of their main characteristics.

4 Complete the mind map about the Zuni people.
Students summarize and organize information from the text in a mind map.

Answers
technique hand carving, *materials* stone, precious gems, coral, shells, other, *examples of animals* mountain lion, bear, coyote, badger, eagle, mole, wolf, *beliefs* have magical powers, protect people

5 🎧⁶ Listen and match each person to the fetish they have.
Students listen to the recording and match each person with the correct fetish.

Answers
left to right 2, 1, 3

Audio Script
1. Allison.
ALLISON: My aunt gave this fetish to me and I carry it in a necklace. I have always liked this animal, it's big and furry. According to the Zuni, this animal is a great protector and healer. Look, it is so beautiful, isn't it?
2. Keith.
KEITH: I got this fetish when I went to New Mexico last year. I bought it because I love this animal. Then later I learned from a Zuni woman that they see this animal as creative and intuitive. That's great, because I'm an artist and creativity and intuition are very important in my work.
3. Joanna.
JOANNA: I have collected fetishes for many, many years. This is my favorite piece, it shows the most important animal for the Zuni. It is associated with personal power, leadership and resourcefulness.

Stop and Think! Value
Are there any animals associated with personality traits in your culture?
- Write on the board a few well-known sayings or comparisons involving animals, for example, *as sly as a fox, an elephant never forgets*, etc. Discuss the ideas behind these sayings.
- Then have students work in groups thinking of personality traits that are associated with certain animals and that are expressed in proverbs, sayings, etc.

Extension
Students research indigenous cultures of North America.
- Organize students into small groups and invite them to carry out research to prepare a presentation about either a) some other aspect of the culture and traditions of the Zuni people or b) the traditions, way of life, art, etc. of some other North American indigenous culture.

Wrap-up
Students discuss their personal responses to the text.
- In small groups, have students share and discuss their responses to the text about fetishes and encourage them to say which fetish figure they most identify with.
- Tell them make a list of four of their favorite celebrities and to say which piece of fetish artwork they would choose as a gift for each celebrity and why.

➠ **(No homework today.)**

 **Project**

Objective
Students will be able to create and carry out a quiz.

Lesson 9   Student's Book pp. 22 and 23

Warm-up
Students play a game to distinguish questions asking for objective facts from those asking for subjective opinions.
- Discuss with students the difference between objective facts and subjective opinions.
- Tell students that you will say some questions, and they should stay seated if the question asks for an objective fact and stand up if the question asks for a subjective opinion.
- Read aloud a series of quiz questions, some concerning facts about the world (*What is the capital of Spain?*), some that ask for factual information about the students themselves (*How old are you?*), and some that ask for students' opinions (*How do you like to spend your free time?*).
- Students who stand up when they should stay seated or vice versa are "out" of the game.

 24

1 Look at the text below and mark (✓) the text type.
Students look at a text and identify what type of text it is.

Answer
a quiz

2 Circle T (True) or F (False).
Students read a personality quiz and determine whether statements about it are true or false.

Answers
1. T, 2. T, 3. F, 4. T

Wrap-up
Students act out skits illustrating the behaviors represented in the quiz.
- Divide students into five groups, one for each quiz question.
- Tell groups to choose one of the answer options for their question and make up a skit to illustrate the personality of someone who would choose that answer on the quiz. The only rule is that they cannot use the exact wording of the answer in their skit.
- Groups perform their skits for the class, and the other groups guess which answer option each group is performing.

🐝 Teaching Tip
Evaluating Group Work
Teenagers usually enjoy working in teams. To ensure that group work goes well, conduct an oral evaluation after a task such as a project in which you ask students to reflect on how much they participated in their group, how they shared tasks, how well they cooperated, how much they listened to the other people on their team, how they made decisions, how they resolved differences of opinion, etc.

Lesson 10 — Student's Book p. 23

Warm-up

Students play Charades to review personality traits vocabulary.
- Write each personality trait on a separate slip of paper (*considerate, friendly, honest, patient, reasonable, responsible*).
- Divide students into teams and have them act out the personality traits for their teams to guess.

3 Work in small groups to create and carry out a quiz.
Students design and create quizzes about personality traits.
- Read aloud the instructions and make sure that students understand the steps that they are to follow.
- Organize students into small groups. Explain that they can use the question format from page 22, but point out also that they can devise their own format if they prefer. As a whole class, brainstorm positive personality traits, questions, and possible answers that students could use.
- Organize students into small groups and have them work on their personality quizzes and the answer options. Make clear that the options should be clearly differentiated to show, for example, evidence of a person being friendly, kind of friendly or unfriendly.

4 Now exchange your quiz with another group. Have them answer your questions while you work on their quiz. Good luck!
Students exchange their personality quizzes with other students and answer them.
- Invite students to answer other students' quizzes and to record their results. Encourage students to compare and discuss their quizzes, including which questions they thought best represented each personality trait.

The Digital Touch
To incorporate digital media in the project, suggest one or more of the following:
- Encourage students to use free online survey and questionnaire tools.
- Have students present their findings from their surveys using PowerPoint or similar slide show presentation programs like Google Slides.
- If possible, allow students to upload their work to the school's website.

Note that students should have the option to do a task on paper or digitally.

Wrap-up

Students compare personality quizzes and vote for their favorites.
- Invite students to vote for their favorites from their classmates' personality quizzes. There can be awards in various categories, e.g., most interesting questions, best interpretation of results, best design, best use of graphics, best use of technology, best overall presentation, etc.

➡ **Workbook p. 128, Activity 1 (Review)**

Review

Objective
Students will be able to consolidate their understanding of the vocabulary and grammar learned in the unit.

Lesson 11   Student's Book p. 24

> ✔ **Homework Check!**
> Workbook p. 128, Activity 1 (Review)
> **Answers**
> **1 Complete the chart.**
> Answers will vary.

Warm-up
Students play a game with adjective prefixes.
- Students form pairs and make a list of funny, incorrect pairings of prefixes and adjectives (like *irhonest, disconsiderate*) and write a sentence using each incorrect adjective.
- Pairs read each other their sentences and use a stopwatch to see how quickly the other pair can identify and correct their adjective prefixes.

1 Complete the chart.
Students complete a chart of adjectives and their opposites.

Answers

Positive, top to bottom honest, reasonable, responsible,
Negative, top to bottom inconsiderate, unfriendly, impatient

2 Look at the scenes. Use adjectives from Activity 1 to describe the people in them.
Students describe people in a scene using personality adjectives.

Answers

1. dishonest, 2. irresponsible, 3. friendly, 4. considerate, 5. patient

Extension
Students find photos of people who match certain personality traits.
- Distribute around the class a selection of magazines and newspapers that contain a good variety of photos of people.
- Organize students into pairs. Then give them a personality trait, for example, *responsible*, and ask each student, working alone, to look for a photo of a person who displays that characteristic. Encourage pairs of students to compare their photos and to discuss their choices.

Wrap-up
Students draw sketches of personal qualities for classmates to guess.
- Play a game of Pictionary in teams. A player from one team draws on the board a picture to represent, for example, the concept of "responsible." As he/she is drawing, players from other teams try to guess which adjective is being drawn.

➡ **(No homework today.)**

> **Teaching Tip**
> **Learning Vocabulary in Word Families**
> Encourage students to record and learn vocabulary items in word families. Taking an example from these pages, students can record *honest, dishonest, honesty, honestly*.

Lesson 12 Student's Book p. 25

Warm-up

Students practice identifying the intonation of tag questions.

- Read aloud a series of tag questions, some with falling intonation (you are pretty sure of the answer) and some with rising intonation (you are not very sure). Ask students to give a thumbs up sign (or something with a similar meaning) when they hear falling intonation and to make a "so so" or "more or less" gesture with their hands when they hear rising intonation. After a few examples, invite students to take turns reading the next sentences with either rising or falling intonation.

3 Circle the correct pronoun.

Students identify the correct pronouns in the tag endings of tag questions.

Answers

1. it, 2. they, 3. she, 4. we, 5. they, 6. I

4 Match the sentences to the tag questions.

Students identify the correct tag question for each sentence.

Answers

1. doesn't he? 2. is he? 3. didn't she? 4. was she? 5. hasn't he? 6. does he? 7. won't she? 8. doesn't she?

5 Write tag questions.

Students complete questions with the correct tag endings.

Answers

1. didn't he? 2. won't he? 3. doesn't she? 4. did she? 5. isn't he? 6. does he? 7. hasn't she? 8. wasn't she?

Big Question

Students are given the opportunity to revisit the Big Question and reflect on it.

- Ask students to turn to the unit opener on page 13 and to look at the photo. Elicit that the girl in the picture is thinking to herself, perhaps thinking about what she is like, that is, what kind of personality she has.

- Discuss with students the question of a person's outward appearance and their inner qualities. Ask them if they think it is possible to know anything about a person's character just from how they look. Write on the board the well-known saying, "You can't judge a book by its cover," and ask students if they think that this is true of people.

- Open another discussion on the subject of why we have the personalities that we do. Ask students whether they believe that some people are simply born dishonest, responsible, impatient, etc. or whether these characteristics are the result of our upbringing and education.

★ Scorecard

Hand out (and/or project) a *Scorecard*. Have students fill in their *Scorecards* for this unit.

➡ **Study for the unit test.**

2 What could I make?

Grammar	Vocabulary
Passive Voice: Nowadays, drone DIY kits <u>are sold</u> on the Internet. Virgin Galactic <u>was founded</u> by Sir Richard Branson. It <u>is being developed</u> by Virgin Galactic.	**Practical Inventions:** drill, glue stick, hammer, hot glue gun, nails, plywood, saw, screw, screwdriver, solder, soldering iron.

Listening	Reading
Listening to instructions	Writing instructions

What could I make?

In the first lesson, read the unit title aloud and have students look carefully at the unit cover. Encourage them to think about the message in the picture. At the end of the unit, students will discuss the big question: *What could I make?*

💭 Teaching Tip
Reflecting on Learning

Invite students to take a little time at the end of each unit in this course to reflect on their learning. Invite them to ask themselves a series of questions about their individual learning process, for example, *How well am I doing? What do I find easy / difficult? What do I need to do more of? How can I improve? What resources can I use? How can my teacher help me?*

 **Vocabulary**

Objective
Students will be able to use **practical inventions** vocabulary to discuss making things.

Lesson 1 — Student's Book pp. 28 and 29

Warm-up
Students brainstorm ideas about *DIY*.
- With books closed, write the letters DIY on the board and ask students if they know what they stand for (Do It Yourself). Elicit that DIY refers to doing activities such as decorating, building and repairing things at home by yourself instead of paying a professional to do it.
- Elicit the names of DIY stores in the local area and ask students if anyone in their family ever does any DIY work around the house.

1 Look at the items below. Organize them in the chart.
Students sort practical inventions vocabulary items into categories.

2 🎧⁷ Now listen and check your answers.
Students listen to check their tables in Activity 1.

Audio Script
Tools
drill, hammer, screwdriver, hot glue gun, soldering iron, saw
Materials
nails, screws, glue stick, solder, plywood

3 Read the sentences and write the item from Activity 1 each one refers to.
Students complete sentences with practical inventions vocabulary.

Answers
1. soldering iron, 2. screw, 3. drill, 4. saw, 5. glue stick, 6. plywood

> **Extension**
> Students create a DIY catalogue.
> - Organize students into small groups and invite them to create a catalogue advertising tools and materials for people interested in DIY projects. Students can cut out photos from magazines and brochures or draw their own illustrations. Have students include short descriptions of each product and prices.

Wrap-up
Students match tools with materials in a mingling activity.
- Have each student take out a piece of paper and assign each a vocabulary word to write on their paper: *solder, soldering iron, screw, screwdriver, glue stick, hot glue gun, nails, hammer, plywood* or *saw*.
- Collect the papers, shuffle them and redistribute, taping one on each student's back.
- Students mingle, asking each other questions about the tool or material on their backs and finding their matches.

 Workbook p. 130, Activities 1 and 2

> 💭 **Teaching Tip**
> **Using Vocabulary Mind Maps**
> Mind maps can be used in various ways, not just for creating a summary of a reading or listening text. Show students how to use mind maps as a way of sorting vocabulary into sets, for example, or as a way of brainstorming ideas for a piece of writing.

Lesson 2   Student's Book p. 29

> ✔ **Homework Check!**
> Workbook p. 130, Activities 1 and 2
> **Answers**
> **1 Complete the sentences using some of the words below.**
> 1. hammer, nails, 2. drill, 3. soldering iron, 4. screws, 5. screwdriver
> **2 Complete the mind maps with the materials and tools you would use in each case.**
> *a broken vase* hot glue gun, glue stick, electricity
> *bookshelves* hammer, saw, plywood, nails, screwdriver, screws

Warm-up
Students review tools and materials vocabulary.
- Read aloud tools and materials items and have students draw simple illustrations of each item. Ask students to check their pictures in pairs.

4 **Look at the items below. Which tools and materials from Activity 1 are used to make them? Write them in your notebook.**
Students identify and note tools and materials used to make certain items.

Answers
A beetle bot solder, soldering iron, screws, screwdriver, drill
A bookcase screws, screwdriver, nails, hammer, drill, plywood, saw

5 🎧 **Listen to Sarah and Matt talking about a DIY project. Circle the tools they mention.**
Students listen for specific information relating to tools and identify the tools mentioned in the conversation.

Answers
hammer, hot glue gun, saw

Audio Script
SARAH: I'm so excited about this DIY project!
MATT: Are you?
SARAH: Let's check the list of materials and tools that we need before we go to the hardware store.
MATT: Are we *really* going over this list *again*?
SARAH: Of course! Just to make sure we don't forget anything…
MATT: OK. So we need plywood… six boards. A pack of nails…
SARAH: Did we include the hammer?
MATT: Yes, the hammer is here… and a saw, too.
SARAH: What about the hot glue gun?
MATT: Why do we need a hot glue gun???
SARAH: To stick these purple and pink butterflies I made from plastic bottles, look!
MATT: OK… so a hot glue gun and five glue sticks. That's it.
SARAH: Great! Let's ask Mom to drive us to the store.

6 🎧 **Listen again and complete the list. Then say which item from Activity 4 Sarah and Matt are planning to make.**
Students listen to complete a list and to identify the item the speakers are planning to make.
- Draw students' attention to the *Guess What!* box. Read the information aloud and discuss why people must use certain protective clothing to stay safe.

Answers
plywood, nails, glue sticks
a bookcase

Stop and Think! Critical Thinking
What are some advantages and disadvantages of recycling and DIY?
- Organize students into small groups and have them discuss some advantages and disadvantages of recycling and DIY. (If necessary, write ideas on the board to get them started.)
- Invite groups to share their comments with the rest of the class.

➡ **Workbook p. 131, Activity 3**

Grammar

Objective
Students will be able to use **passive voice** to discuss inventions.

Lesson 3 Student's Book pp. 30 and 31

✔ **Homework Check!**
Workbook p. 131, Activity 3

Answers
3 Find and write the past participle of each verb to make a passive form.
1. been, 2. invented, 3. made, 4. developed, 5. used, 6. announced, 7. shown, 8. invited, 9. written, 10. taken

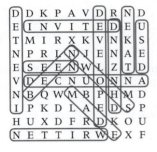

Warm-up
Students draw and describe their own spaceships.
- Invite students to sketch their own ideas about what they imagine spaceships for space tourism will be like in the future. Have them share their ideas with the rest of the class.

1 Read the texts. Which invention is the oldest?
Students skim a series of texts to find key dates.

Answer
the remote control system

2 Underline the passive voice forms in the text.
Students identify passive voice forms in a text.
- Draw students' attention to the box with information about Active Voice and **Passive Voice** and clarify any doubts that students may have. Remind them that the passive voice is used in various verb tenses.

Answers
is called, are known, were developed, have been used, are sold, can be built, are being used, will be used, is being developed, was founded, will be carried, will be experienced, have been sold

3 Read the headlines. Write *A* if the verb is in the active form, or *P* if it is in the passive form.
Students sort news headlines according to their use of active or passive forms.

Answers
left to right, top to bottom P, A, P, P, A, A

Extension
Students research famous inventions and their inventors.
- Ask students to work in small groups researching some famous inventions. In each case, have them use the passive voice to say who it was invented by.

Wrap-up
Students answer true/false quiz questions about texts.
- Divide the class into two teams. Read aloud a series of statements, some true and some false, about the inventors and inventions in the text on this page. Say, for example, *Drones were developed after World War I* (false).
- The teams take turns answering *true* or *false*. They get one point for each correct answer and an additional point if they can correct a false statement.

 Workbook p. 131, Activity 1

💭 Teaching Tip
Using Grammatical Terms
Students will find it useful to be familiar with grammatical concepts such as the difference between the *simple* and the *continuous* forms of verbs. Use these terms in your explanations of grammar.

Lesson 4 Student's Book p. 31

> ✔ **Homework Check!**
> Workbook p. 131, Activity 1
> **Answers**
> **1 Label each sentence as *A* (Active) or *P* (Passive). Underline the active or passive verb.**
> 1. A, invented, 2. A, created, 3. P, was created, 4. A, is improving, 5. P, has been improved, 6. A, are using, 7. P, is being used, 8. P, is being developed, 9. A, is developing

Warm-up
Students review the form of passive voice structures.
- Give students a quick-fire test of the past participles of various verbs, including irregular verbs, for example, *found, sold, made*.
- Divide the class into two or more teams and have each team line up at the board. One student from each team goes to the board at a time.
- Say the base form of a verb and have the students at the board race to provide the correct past participle.

4 Complete the sentences with the passive form of the verbs.
Students complete sentences with the correct passive voice verb forms using cues.

Answers
1. are made, 2. can be found, 3. are being used, 4. has been developed, 5. will be sent

5 Match the items in the columns to write sentences in the passive voice in your notebook.
Students form passive voice sentences from prompts.

Answers
1. Apple was started by Steve Jobs, Steve Wozniak and Ronald Wayne in 1976. 2. Smartphones are used to surf the Internet by millions of people nowadays. 3. Helicopters were invented in the first half of the 20th century. 4. The World Wide Web was developed by Tim Berners-Lee in 1989. He also invented the web browser.

6 Think Fast! Work with a partner. Write two newspaper headlines in the passive voice, similar to the ones in Activity 3.
Students do a three-minute timed challenge: they write newspaper headlines using the passive voice.
- Ask students to work in pairs writing two newspaper headlines in the passive voice, using the ones in Activity 3 as examples.

Extension
Students transform active sentences to passive and vice versa.
- Give students a series of sentences, some in the active voice and some in the passive voice. Be sure to use a variety of verb tenses. Ask students to transform the active sentences to passive and vice versa.

Wrap-up
Students role-play presentations about fictitious inventions.
- Invite students to give presentations in which they take on the role of inventors and explain how their wonderful new invention was created. This could be something as simple as a pen or a ruler, but students can make up special properties and features, for example, *This pen was designed to be used in space. A Bluetooth connection was included in this ruler to send measurements to your phone.*

➡ **Workbook p. 132, Activity 2**

Listening & Writing

Objective
Students will be able to listen to instructions and write instructions.

Lesson 5   Student's Book p. 32

> ✔ **Homework Check!**
> Workbook p. 132, Activity 2
> **Answers**
> **2 Read the text and circle the correct option.**
> 1. is known, 2. is located, 3. was born, 4. was influenced, 5. was founded, 6. was incorporated, 7. was chosen, 8. was built, 9. was used

Warm-up
Students review imperatives by coming up with instructions for fixing something.
- Students form small groups. Give each group an example of something that needs repair or improvement, for example, *the light isn't turning on, we don't have enough room for all of our books* or *the water in the sink won't drain*.
- Tell groups to come up with a solution to the problem (which can be practical or silly), and develop the steps that should be taken to fix the problem.
- Groups present their problem and solution to the class.

1 Do you know what a hack is? Read the definition and find out.
Students discuss a contemporary use of the term *hack*.
- Ask students to discuss this modern definition. You may wish to contrast the noun *hack* with the verb *to hack* and the noun *hacker*, commonly heard nowadays in relation to data held on computers.

2 Look at the hack below and discuss with a classmate what kind of problem it solves.
Students look at a simple life hack and discuss what it does.

3 🎧⁹ Listen and confirm your guess in Activity 2.
Students listen to confirm their ideas about the life hack in the previous activity.

Audio Script
MELINDA: Hi guys! This is Melinda, your host on *What Hack Is It?*, your weekly podcast with hacks and DIY tips to make your life easier.
Today, I'm going to teach you how to make a very, very simple hack to solve a big problem. You're throwing a party at your house and, you know, music is essential at parties, isn't it? All your favorite songs are on your smartphone, but there are no cables to connect it to a loudspeaker or to another sound device. So what can you do? You can make speakers for your smartphone using simple, everyday materials you can find at home. It's gonna take you less than ten minutes, believe me.

Wrap-up
Students brainstorm lists of everyday materials that can be used to make life hacks.
- Organize students into small groups and have them brainstorm lists of everyday, reusable objects such as disposable cups, plastic straws, paper towel rolls, metal cans, plastic bottles, egg boxes, yogurt containers, jam jars, etc.
- Have each group choose two items and invent something that could be made from them.
- Collect the lists for use in the next lesson.

➡ **Workbook p. 133, Activity 1**

Lesson 6   Student's Book pp. 32 and 33

> ✔ Homework Check!
> Workbook p. 133, Activity 1
> **Answers**
> **1 Read the text and circle *T* (True) or *F* (False).**
> 1. F, 2. T, 3. T, 4. F, 5. T

Warm-up
Students develop a DIY project.
- Students form the same groups they worked in for the Wrap-up in the previous lesson.
- Cut the lists of reusable items from the previous lesson into strips, fold them and place them in a bowl or other container. Tell each group to send a representative to choose three slips from the container.
- Using the items picked at random, groups develop a DIY project. Have students identify tools needed for their project and present their ideas to the class.

4 🎧¹⁰ **Order the steps to make the hack. Then listen and check your answers.**
Students listen and order the steps in a process.

Answers
top to bottom, left to right 3, 8, 7, 1, 6, 9, 2, 4, 5

Audio Script
MELINDA: The steps are very easy to follow. And there's a fully illustrated, step-by-step guide on our website.
NARRATOR: One
MELINDA: First, you need to gather the materials and tools. You're gonna need two plastic cups, a paper towel roll, a utility knife, a ruler and a marker.
NARRATOR: Two
MELINDA: Once you have the materials and tools, off to work! The ruler is used to measure the perimeter of the exterior part of your smartphone. Write down the size on a piece of paper.
NARRATOR: Three
MELINDA: Next, use the marker to draw a rectangle the size of the smartphone on the paper towel roll. Draw it in the center of the roll.
NARRATOR: Four
MELINDA: Then a hole is made on the roll using the utility knife, according to the outline of the rectangle.
NARRATOR: Five
MELINDA: Cut only three sides of the rectanglle. The fourth side is left as a flap to support your phone.
NARRATOR: Six
MELINDA: Now that the paper roll is ready, it is time to make the speakers! Use the marker once again, this time to trace circles using the roll as a shape.
NARRATOR: Seven
MELINDA: Cut the circles out of the plastic cup using the utility knife.
NARRATOR: Eight
MELINDA: After that, fit the paper towel roll into the plastic cups with the hole in the roll facing upwards. You can decorate your hack anyway you want—markers, spray paint or stickers can be used to make it beautiful.
NARRATOR: Nine
MELINDA: Finally, place your smartphone in the hole in the paper towel roll. Then just choose your favorite tune, turn it up and enjoy the music!

5 Order the steps.
Students number the steps in a process.

Answers
left to right, top to bottom 1, 3, 2, 4

6 Now use the prompts to write the complete instructions. Refer to the *Be Strategic!* box.
Students write complete instructions using connector expressions.
- Draw students' attention to the **Be Strategic!** box and ask them to read the information. Remind students to use these connecting words to mark the steps in a sequence.

Answers
Answers will vary.

Wrap-up
Students write instructions for their own hacks.
- Have students work in pairs writing complete instructions for the DIY project their group developed at the beginning of the lesson. Tell pairs to feel free to improve or change the project as they wish.

▶ **Workbook p. 133, Activity 2**

Preparing for the Next Lesson
Ask students to watch an introduction to Kelvin Doe:
http://goo.gl/kYREhf

 Culture

Objectives
Students will be able to learn about a young inventor.

Lesson 7 Student's Book pp. 34 and 35

> ✔ **Homework Check!**
> Workbook p. 133, Activity 2
> **Answers**
> 2 Think of an invention and write a paragraph about it in your notebook.
> Answers will vary.

 36

Warm-up
Students develop their inventions in groups.
- Have students form small groups and share the inventions they wrote about for their homework.
- Tell groups to imagine that they are a company that will manufacture and sell the invention. Have groups choose the invention they would like to manufacture, make improvements to it, and present their plan to the class.

1 Look at the pictures. Discuss with a classmate how you think they are related to Kelvin Doe, a young inventor.
Students look at images and discuss ways in which that may be connected to an individual.
- Draw students' attention to the *Guess What!* box. Discuss the information in the box as a whole class.

2 Now read a fact sheet about Kelvin. Order the paragraphs in the text.
Students number the paragraphs in a text in the correct order.

Answers
top to bottom 2, 1, 5, 3, 4

3 Were your ideas about Kelvin in Activity 1 right? Read the biography again, if necessary.
Students discuss their initial ideas about a person in light of new information.
- Organize students into pairs and have them discuss their initial ideas about the subject of the text (based on the images) with their impressions now that they have read the fact sheet. Elicit observation and comment.

Wrap-up
Students write passive voice sentences about the life and work of Kelvin Doe.
- Have students work in pairs formulating five passive voice sentences about Kelvin Doe's life and work. Give them a sample sentence to get them started, for example, *Kelvin's house and his neighbors' cell phones were powered by a generator.* Ask students to share their sentences and to underline the passive voice structure in each one.

➡ **(No homework today.)**

 Teaching Tip

Being Curious About Other Cultures
When students travel abroad in the future, apart from meeting native speakers of English, they will also meet many non-native speakers from a wide range of countries. Encourage students to be curious about people from other places and to always be sensitive to other people's cultures and traditions.

Lesson 8 Student's Book p. 35

Warm-up
Students recap facts about the subject of the fact sheet.
- With books closed, ask students a series of quick-fire quiz questions to test their memory of the fact sheet about Kelvin Doe, for example, *When was he born?* (1996), *Where was he born?* (Sierra Leone), *How did he learn engineering and electronics?* (he taught himself), etc.

◀ **Write the milestones in Kelvin's life in the appropriate place on his timeline.**
Students complete a timeline with key events in a person's life, drawn from the text in Activity 2.

Answers

2, 4, 6, 1, 3, 5

Stop and Think! Value
Do you know any young person in your country who came up with simple and cheap solutions for everyday problems?
- Organize students into small groups and have them discuss any young people from their country who came up with simple and cheap solutions for everyday problems. (If necessary, write ideas on the board to get them started.)
- Invite groups to share their comments with the rest of the class.

> **Extension**
> Students brainstorm a list of problems in their communities that need to be solved.
> - Organize students into small groups and have them come up with a list of problems or issues that they think need to be addressed in their local community. These might be about education, health, employment, safety, sports and recreation, culture and the arts, transportation, access to the Internet, etc.

Wrap-up
Students role-play an interview with Kelvin Doe.
- Organize students into pairs and invite them to role-play a conversation between a newspaper reporter and Kelvin Doe talking about his life and work.
- Encourage students to share their role plays with the rest of the class.

▶ **(No homework today.)**

Project

Objective
Students will be able to invent and present a life hack.

Lesson 9 — Student's Book pp. 36 and 37

Wrap-up
Students answer survey questions about life hacks.
- Carry out a simple, show-of-hands survey to find out about students' knowledge of household matters. For example, ask them if they know any tricks for getting stains out of clothes, or if they know of an original way to reuse some everyday item instead of throwing it out with the trash.
- Encourage students to share their ideas with the rest of the class.

1 Read this text about life hacking. Did you know about these life hack ideas?
Students read a text and discuss their initial reactions to it.
- Ask students to just look at the text. Elicit ideas about what kind of text it is and where it might be found. Then ask students to read the text more carefully. Discuss the question in the title of the text and, in particular, ask students to say if they have heard of these life hack ideas.
- Ask a series of questions to check students' understanding of the text. For example, ask, *How does the fresh egg hack work? How does it help people? How does the pen spring prevent a phone charger from breaking?*

2 Work in small groups and come up with a life hack. Follow the steps below.
Students work in groups inventing life hacks.
- Ask students to look carefully at the four-step instructions. Focus their attention in particular on the tips, which will help them to avoid wasting time with problems that are too big for them to solve or which simply cannot be solved.
- Have students work together coming up with a problem that needs solving, why it bothers them, what their life hack solution is, what recycled, everyday materials are used to make their life hack and how to construct it.

Wrap-up
Students invent names for a life hack website.
- Organize students into small teams and issue them the challenge of coming up with a good name for a website dedicated to life hacks.
- Pool all the names and invite students to vote for their favorites.

Teaching Tip
Relating Lessons to Real Life
Try to show students how their lessons relate to real life. If they feel that lessons are relevant to them personally, students will be more engaged in class.

Lesson 10 Student's Book p. 37

Wrap-up

Students review their life hacks in their project groups.
- To help students prepare for their presentations, have them discuss answers to questions about their life hacks.
- Write a few questions on the board, for example, *What percentage of students in our class have probably experienced this problem? Is another solution to the problem available? Why is your solution the best one?*

3 Now present your life hack to the class.
Students present their life hacks to their classmates.

Stop and Think! Critical Thinking
Which life hack was the most interesting? Why?
- Organize students into small groups and have them discuss which of the life hacks that their classmates presented was the most interesting and why.

> **The Digital Touch**
> To incorporate digital media in the project, suggest one or more of the following:
> - Encourage students to use free video editing programs and tools to make practical demonstration videos of their life hacks and post these on safe video-sharing sites.
> - Have students present their life hacks using PowerPoint or similar slide show presentation programs.
> - If possible, allow students to upload their work to the school's website.
>
> Note that students should have the option to do a task on paper or digitally.

Extension
Students prepare a pamphlet of school hacks as a guide for new students.
- Organize students into small groups and have them design and create a pamphlet containing useful school hacks to help students who are new to the school.
- Invite students to display and share their pamphlets around the school.

Wrap-up
Students invent "mock" life hacks.
- Organize students into pairs and invite them to come up with "mock" life hacks, that is, life hacks for problems that are not really problems or inconveniences at all, for example, a way to save a tiny amount of energy when using the remote control for the TV, a way to make it easier to take toast out of a toaster, etc.
- Have pairs share their ideas with the class. The class votes on the funniest or most absurd life hacks.

➡ **Workbook p. 132, Activity 1 (Review)**

Review

Objectives
Students will be able to consolidate their understanding of the vocabulary and grammar learned in the unit.

Lesson 11 — Student's Book p. 38

> ✔ Homework Check!
> Workbook p. 132, Activity 1 (Review)
> **Answers**
> **1 Complete each sentence with the correct passive form. Then match.**
> 1. was invented, d, 2. are called, c, 3. was developed, e, 4. is used, f, 5. was made, a

Warm-up
Students play Charades to review materials and tools vocabulary.
- Divide the class into teams and have students act out the use of a material or tool for their teammates to guess the vocabulary word.

1 Which tools are these? Look and label.
Students identify and label DIY tools shown in photos.

Answers
1. soldering iron, 2. screwdriver, 3. saw, 4. hot glue gun, 5. hammer, 6. drill

2 Label the pictures. Then complete the chart with the tools in Activity 1 the materials are commonly used with.
Students identify and label photos and then match DIY materials with the correct tools.

Answers
top to bottom, left to right nails, hammer, plywood, saw, screws, screwdriver, glue sticks, hot glue gun, solder, soldering iron

3 Correct the mistakes in the sentences.
Students read and correct sentences about the use of materials and tools.

Answers
1. ~~drill~~ Let's find a <u>hammer</u> to knock these nails into the plywood. 2. ~~solder~~ Can you get me a screwdriver? I want to remove this <u>screw</u>. 3. ~~nails~~ I'm going to the office supply store downtown. I need to buy <u>glue sticks</u> for my hot glue gun. 4. ~~saw~~ Emily wants to use a <u>drill</u> to make a hole in the wall, but she has never done it.

4 Which materials or tools have you already worked with? Write two examples in your notebook. Say what you used them for.
Students write about tools that they have used themselves.
- Recap the materials and tools on this page and elicit some suggestions for the types of DIY projects that people typically do using these materials and tools, for example, plywood, hammer, nails—putting up shelves in a garage.
- Ask students to write at least two examples of times when they used various DIY materials and tools to make something.

Wrap-up
Students share "DIY Disaster" stories.
- Organize students into pairs and invite them to share real or invented anecdotes about DIY projects that went disastrously wrong.
- Invite students to share their stories with the rest of the class and then ask students to vote for the story that they found the funniest, the most original, etc.

➡ **(No homework today.)**

Lesson 12 Student's Book p. 39

Wrap-up

Students brainstorm the names of national monuments from different countries.

- Organize students into teams. Set a stopwatch for three minutes and tell groups to compile a list of ten countries and famous monuments that are national symbols of those countries, for example, *France: The Eiffel Tower*. For each monument, ask students to estimate or guess the year in which it was built. Have students save their lists for later.

5 Are these sentences in the active or passive voice? In the passive sentences, circle the agent, if it is mentioned.

Students identify and analyze active and passive voice sentences.

Answers

1. Active, 2. Passive, (Martin Cooper) 3. Passive, (swimmers), (10-year-old-boy), 4. Active

6 Transform the active sentences into passive ones.

Students complete passive voice sentences with the correct form of the verbs to make the meaning match that of the active voice sentence.

Answers

1. was recycled, 2. was used, was called, 3. Was Microsoft founded, 4. drones will be used

7 Complete the sentences with the passive voice of the verbs. Then match the sentences to the pictures they describe.

Students complete the sentences with the correct passive voice form of the verb in parentheses and then match them with pictures.

Answers

1. was invented, 2. has been sold, 3. was designed, was located, 4. was created, was made
left to right 4, 1, 3, 2

> **Extension**
>
> Students prepare posters about famous national monuments.
>
> - Ask students to work in the same teams they were in for the Warm-up activity. Ask them to research the dates of construction of the national monuments on their lists and to use this information with any other facts they find to create an informational poster with photos or drawings and captions in the passive voice. For example, next to a photo of the Eiffel Tower, the caption would read, *The Eiffel Tower was constructed in 1889. It was designed by Gustave Eiffel.*

Big Question

Students are given the opportunity to revisit the Big Question and reflect on it.

- Ask students to turn to the unit opener on page 27 and to look at the collage of photos. Elicit observation and comment about the photos.
- Focusing attention on the young woman in the top right-hand photo, you may wish to explore traditional attitudes versus modern views regarding women's participation in the fields of science and engineering.
- Regarding the photo of the egg carton, discuss the importance of recycling materials and either reusing them or repurposing them.

Scorecard

Hand out (and/or project) a *Scorecard*. Have students fill in their *Scorecards* for this unit.

➡ **Study for the unit test.**

3 How am I different now?

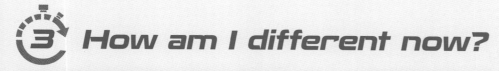

Grammar	Vocabulary
Present Perfect and Present Perfect Continuous: I've seen Piazza San Marco and the Bridge of Sighs. I've been enjoying this adventure by myself! **Since / For:** I've been eating a lot of Italian food since I arrived here. I've been touring around Italy for two weeks now.	**Milestones:** attend acting classes, build a drone, create a vlog, develop a computer game, get a part-time job, learn another language, start a band with friends, write a book

Reading	Speaking
Predicting content	Talking about a life-changing experience

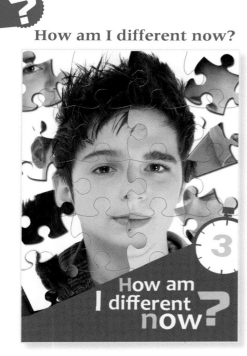

In the first lesson, read the unit title aloud and have students look carefully at the unit cover. Encourage them to think about the message in the picture. At the end of the unit, students will discuss the big question: *How am I different now?*

Teaching Tip
Making Mistakes and Learning
Some students feel anxious about making mistakes and this can affect their self-confidence and their willingness to take part in class. Explain to students that mistakes are an unavoidable and also a necessary part of language learning. Identifying and analyzing the mistaken form of a word or a structure and then comparing it to the correct form is a very good way to learn.

 Vocabulary

Objective
Students will be able to use **milestones vocabulary** to talk about life experiences and life histories.

Lesson 1   Student's Book pp. 42 and 43

Warm-up
Students compare older and recent photos of the same individual.
- Show students photos of celebrities when they were young and now and invite observation and comment about how the people have changed physically.
- Alternatively, invite students to bring in photos of themselves when they were young children.

 44

1 Complete the captions with the words from the box.
Students complete the captions for a series of images.
- Draw students' attention to the *Guess What!* box. Read the information aloud and discuss some well-known examples of people who achieve great success at a very young age.

Answers

top to bottom, left to right computer game, foreign language, book, abroad alone, acting classes, part-time job, band with your friends *next page (43)* vlog, drone

2 🎧 Listen to a presentation of the results of a survey. Match the colors with the activities.
Students listen and match the color on a pie chart with a series of activities.

Answers

top to bottom creating a vlog, traveling abroad alone, getting a part-time job, learning a foreign language, starting a band with friends

Audio Script
As you all know, we carried out a survey with our magazine readers about activities they would like to do, according to the suggestions in our feature "Activities that Can Change Your Life!" We selected the five most popular activities among the answers. The top activity, chosen by 32% of our readers, is "traveling abroad alone." This didn't come as a big surprise, because we know that traveling is one of our readers' favorite activities.
In the second place, we have "starting a band with friends." It's interesting to see that so many readers are interested in music: a total of 26%.
Next, with 20%, we have "learning a foreign language." It's a shame we don't know which languages our readers would like to learn. Is it the classic French or the emergent Chinese Mandarin?
In fourth place, with 15%, we have "getting a part-time job." We thought more readers would be interested in working—maybe they're more focused on having fun?
And finally, we have "creating a vlog," with 7%. Vlogs have become really popular lately, but it seems our readers are more interested in watching content instead of creating their own.
Any questions?

Wrap-up
Students review the script of the audio track.
- Provide students with copies of the script for the audio recording and invite them to practice reading it aloud as if it were a report on the radio.

➡ **Workbook p. 134, Activities 1 and 2**

Lesson 2 Student's Book p. 43

✔ **Homework Check!**

Workbook p. 134, Activities 1 and 2

Answers

1 Read the prompts and write the name of the activity. Use the words in the box.
1. Travel abroad alone. 2. Get a part-time job.
3. Create a vlog. 4. Learn a foreign language.
5. Write a book.

2 Match the parts of the sentence. Then number the pictures each sentence refers to.
1. f, 2. e, 3. c, 4. d, 5. a; *left to right, top to bottom*
4, 2, 5, 1, 3

Warm-up

Students review vocabulary for talking about life experiences.
- Read aloud some definitions of key vocabulary items from the previous page and have students supply the correct terms, for example, in a foreign country or countries (abroad), a remote-controlled pilotless aircraft or missile (drone), a form of blog for which the medium is video (vlog).

3 Complete the chart with the activities on page 42.

Students complete a chart about life experiences.

Answers

Answers will vary.

4 Now share your ideas from Activity 3 with a friend. Explain your choices.

Students share experiences and opinions from the previous activity.

Stop and Think! Critical Thinking

Which of the activities in this lesson would have the most impact on a teenager's future? Why?
- Organize students into small groups and have them discuss which activities would have the most impact. (If necessary, write ideas on the board to get them started.)
- Invite groups to share their comments with the rest of the class.

> ### Extension
> Students share suggestions about where and how young people can gain experience in the activities featured in Activity 1.
> - Organize students into small groups and have them share and discuss ideas about the places in their town or city where young people can take acting classes, for example, or ways in which they can try activities like starting a band.

Wrap-up

Students review and expand vocabulary from Activity 1.
- Write on the board certain phrases from Activity 1, for example, *Develop your own computer game, Attend acting classes, Learn a language,* etc.
- Organize students into teams and challenge them to come up with as many alternative phrases as they can using the same verbs, for example, *Attend music lessons, Build your own bicycle,* etc.

▶ **Workbook p. 135, Activity 3**

Objectives
Students will be able to use **present perfect, present perfect continuous** and *since / for* to talk about life experiences.

Lesson 3 Student's Book pp. 44 and 45

✔ **Homework Check!**
Workbook p. 135, Activity 3

Answers
3 Write the activities you would recommend for each person. Use the words from Activity 1.
1. Attend acting classes. 2. Develop a computer game. 3. Build a drone. 4. Get a part-time job.
5. Travel abroad alone.

Warm-up
Students play a mime game to review vocabulary.
- Organize students into two teams. Have students from one team mime one of the activities from the previous pages for the other team to guess.

1 Read the blog posts. Which activities from the Vocabulary section do they refer to?
Students read blog posts and identify key information.

Answers
1. Traveling abroad alone, 2. Getting a part-time job

2 Underline the present perfect form and circle the present perfect continuous form in the blog posts.
Students identify specific verb structures in a text.
- Draw students' attention to the box with information about the *Present Perfect vs. Present Perfect Continuous* and clarify any doubts that students may have about form or meaning. Remind them that continuous verb forms refer to actions that are in progress.

Answers
present perfect 1. I've seen, I haven't packed, I've taken, 2. I've done, things haven't been, they've been, I've imagined, I've written, have sent it, I've only had, Alice has also given me
present perfect continuous 1. I have been touring, I've been enjoying, I have been visiting, I've been eating, 2. I've been practicing, She's been working, I've been checking

3 Complete the sentences. Use the present perfect continuous.
Students complete present perfect continuous sentences from picture prompts.

Answers
1. have been running, 2. has been learning,
3. has been recording, 4. have been attending

Wrap-up
Students invent additional information about the people in Activity 3.
- Have students reread the completed captions in the previous activity. Ask them to write one more sentence about each of the people in the photos, using the present perfect continuous and a different verb. Have students share their ideas with the rest of the class.

➡ **Workbook pp. 135 and 136, Activities 1 and 2**

 Teaching Tip
Making Grammar Posters
When students have understood a grammatical structure, they can usually explain it to others. Invite students to create posters illustrating the form and meaning of the present perfect and the present perfect continuous. Display their posters around the classroom. Repeat this with other grammatical structures that students study later on.

Lesson 4 — Student's Book p. 45

> ✔ **Homework Check!**
> Workbook pp. 135 and 136, Activities 1 and 2
> **Answers**
> **1 Read and label the actions as finished or still in progress.**
> 1. finished, 2. finished, 3. still in progress, 4. still in progress, 5. finished
> **2 Complete the sentences using the present perfect continuous.**
> 1. has been building, 2. haven't been practicing, 3. has been developing, 4. haven't been writing

Warm-up

Students play a team game to practice the present perfect.
- Students plan and mark on a map the route of a trip around Europe, for example. They then choose one of the places on their route for the other team to guess. The other team asks, *Have you been to _____?* and are told, *Yes, we have.* or, *No, not yet.* or, *No, we aren't planning to go there.* until the other team guesses exactly where they are now.

4 🎧¹² **Listen to four conversations. Are the actions finished, or are they still in progress?**
Students listen to conversations and analyze the meaning of each one.

Answers
1. finished, 2. in progress, 3. in progress, 4. in progress

Audio Script

One
Boy 1: So, have you built this drone yourself, Savannah?
Girl 1: Yes, I have. Isn't it amazing, Charley?
Boy 1: It sure is! Congratulations!

Two
Girl 2: I've heard you're writing a book, Logan. Is that right?
Boy 2: Yeah, but it is really tough… It's a fantasy novel.
Girl 2: I see… How long have you been working on it?
Boy 2: For three years…
Girl 2: Wow… I bet it's gonna be a looong book.

Three
Girl 3: How long has Julia been traveling?
Boy 3: Let me see… She's been traveling for two weeks now, I guess.
Girl 3: And where's she?
Boy 3: She's in Italy. Look at these pictures she posted on her photo social network profile…
Girl 3: Oh, they're beautiful!

Four
Girl 4: What have you been doing lately, Sean?
Boy 4: Me? Nothing much. I've been playing with my band every weekend and…
Girl 4: Wait! Do you have a band?
Boy 4: Yes, I do… I play the drums, actually.
Girl 4: How come you never told me that!

5 Complete the sentences with the present perfect or the present perfect continuous.
Students complete sentences with the correct verb forms.

Answers
1. been studying, 2. finished baking, 3. have you been practicing, 4. haven't seen them

6 Think Fast! Write a comment for each blog post in Activity 1.
Students do a two-minute timed challenge: they write comments on a blog.

Wrap-up

Students make up variations on a story.
- Invite students to make up variations on the Goldilocks and the Three Bears story with modern ideas such as, *Someone has been using my telephone!*, and to use them to improvise a new version of the story.

▶ **Workbook p. 136, Activities 3 and 4**

Reading & Speaking

Objectives
Students will be able to predict content and talk about a life-changing experience.

Lesson 5   Student's Book pp. 46 and 47

> ✔ **Homework Check!**
> Workbook p. 136, Activities 3 and 4
> **Answers**
> **3 Read and circle the correct verbs.**
> 1. has been traveling abroad alone, 2. has built, 3. has written, 4. has been developing
> **4 Complete the sentences using** *since* **or** *for*.
> 1. for, 2. for, 3. since, 4. for

Warm-up
Students play a guessing game about professions to practice the present perfect continuous.
- Organize students into teams. One team describes its recent activities using the present perfect continuous, for example, *I have been visiting construction sites all day. I have been talking to builders all morning.* The other team tries to guess the profession (architect).

1 Read the title of the article and its lead. Then look at the photos and the map. What do you think it is about?
Students predict the content of a text from visual clues.
- Draw students' attention to the **Be Strategic!** box and ask them to read the information. Remind students to use titles, subheadings, photos, maps, charts, etc. to help them predict what a text is about.

2 Now read the article to check your predictions in Activity 1.
Students check their predictions.

3 Read the article again. Mark (✓) YES, NO or NOT MENTIONED for the statements below.
Students read a text for detailed information.
Answers
1. YES, 2. NO (She was 10 years old.), 3. YES, 4. NO (The Dutch government was against her solo journey.), 5. NOT MENTIONED, 6. NOT MENTIONED

4 How do you think Laura's life changed after her solo sailing? Discuss with a partner.
Students discuss their reactions to the text.

Extension
Students prepare oral presentations about young adventurers.
- Have students work in small groups researching and preparing oral presentations about young adventurers such as, for example, Jordan Romero, the youngest person to climb Mount Everest.

Wrap-up
Students role-play interviews.
- Have students work in pairs role-playing a radio interview with Laura Dekker.

 Workbook p. 137, Activity 1

Teaching Tip
Managing Fast Finishers
Some students complete activities more quickly than others, so it's a good idea to have a few extra activities on hand, otherwise these students may become bored and disruptive. One set of activities designed for fast finishers are the *Just for Fun* pages. Students can work on these individually and then check their answers in the back of the Student's Book. The *Just for Fun* activities for this unit are on page 54.

Lesson 6 — Student's Book p. 47

> ✔ **Homework Check!**
> Workbook p. 137, Activity 1
> **Answers**
> **1 Read and correct the false statements below.**
> 3. A teen can contribute to the household or to their own expenses with the money earned from a part-time job. 4. Whether a part-time job is right or not depends on the particular teenager and his or her situation.

Warm-up
Students recall facts about the article on the previous page.
- Read out some incomplete statements about Laura Dekker's voyage around the world and ask students to complete each one with the correct information. For example, *Laura Dekker was born in New Zealand in…* (1995).

5 🎧¹³ **Now listen to a conversation about another life-changing experience. Then circle T (True) or F (False).**
Students listen for specific information to determine whether each statement about the conversation is true or false.

Answers
1. F, 2. F, 3. T

Audio Script
MADISON: That was a great training, Matt! But nothing compared to the marathons you run!
MATT: You're great company, Madison.
MADISON: Tell me, Matt, how long have you been running marathons?
MATT: Let me see… For two years now, I guess.
MADISON: And why did you start?
MATT: It all started at a fund-raising marathon for children with cancer. My little brother had leukemia at the time, and I decided to run in order to help gather money for the hospital where he was being treated.
MADISON: Oh… I see. But did you run a marathon before that?
MATT: No! Never! I trained for three months only, but I completed the race.
MADISON: Wow! And how many marathons have you run since then?
MATT: Six… and I'll run another one in two weeks.
MADISON: And how has running marathons changed your life?
MATT: It has shown me that I can overcome my limits. I'm a much more confident person. I'm also healthier and have made new friends.

6 🎧¹³ **Listen again. Then match the questions from the conversations to their meaning.**
Students match sentences with their meanings.

Answers
top to bottom 2, 3, 1, 4

7 Take notes in your notebook about a life-changing experience. You can also imagine one. Use the chart below.
Students write notes about a life-changing experience.

Answers
Answers will vary.

8 Now take turns sharing the experience with a classmate. Use the questions in Activity 6.
Students share their experiences in pairs.

Wrap-up
Students play a True or False game.
- Invite students to share three experiences, one of them true and two of them false. Other students try to guess which is the true experience.

➡ **Workbook p. 137, Activity 2**

Preparing for the Next Lesson
Ask students to watch an introduction to the science of tsunamis: goo.gl/A6KWoH or invite them to consult the following website: goo.gl/DyXhr2

 Culture

Objective
Students will be able to talk about the 2004 Indian Ocean tsunami.

Lesson 7 Student's Book pp. 48 and 49

> ✔ **Homework Check!**
> Workbook p. 137, Activity 2
> **Answers**
> 2 In your notebook, write about a part-time job you want to have.
> Answers will vary.

▶ 50 **Warm-up**
Students review and share facts about natural disasters.
- Elicit the names of natural disasters (earthquakes, hurricanes, volcanic eruptions, floods, landslides, forest fires, etc.) and ask students to share some basic facts that they can recall.

1 How much do you know about the 2004 Indian Ocean tsunami? Write key words in the chart below. You can look at the pictures for some ideas.
Students brainstorm facts about the 2004 Indian Ocean tsunami.

2 Read the information below and confirm your guesses.
Students read a short text to confirm their answers.

3 ¹⁴ Listen to a podcast and mark (✓) the sentences that are true.
Students listen for specific information and mark the sentences that are true.

Answers
2, 3, 6

Audio Script
NARRATOR: Tilly Smith was only 10 years old when her life changed forever. She was in Phuket Island, in Thailand, spending the end-of-the-year holidays with her father, mother and little sister.
It was a beautiful but cloudy morning. Tilly and her family were walking along Mai Khao beach, right in front of their hotel, when Tilly realized something was really, really wrong.
YOUNG WOMAN: The sea was high on the sand. The waves were coming in, but they were not going out. There was too much froth on the waves. I thought, "I've seen this, I've seen this somewhere." Then I remembered a geography class when my teacher told us about the signs of tsunamis and realized something terrible was going to happen.
I started shouting, "Tsunami, there's going to be a tsunami!" My parents had no idea what I was talking about. My mom didn't believe me. Finally, my dad and I talked to a security guard at our hotel. He was Japanese, and pretty familiar with tsunamis. He said, "I think she's right!"
NARRATOR: The guard warned the tourists and hotel staff on the beach to leave immediately and look for protection in high places inside the hotel. Just minutes later, a huge wave hit the beach and the hotel.
YOUNG WOMAN: No one on our beach died, but thousands of people perished in Thailand. My dad was just in shock. He kept saying, "What if we hadn't listened to you?"

> **Extension**
> Students prepare posters about tsunamis.
> - Organize students into groups and have them research and create posters that explain how tsunamis happen and the effects that they can have.

Wrap-up
Students create tsunami-themed crosswords.
- Invite students to make crosswords using tsunami-related vocabulary, for example, *disaster, earthquake, magnitude, coastal, beach, waves, froth*, etc.

▶ **(No homework today.)**

> 🐝 **Teaching Tip**
> **Researching Real People**
> Encourage students to find out more about the lives of real people featured in their books, people like Laura Dekker and Tilly Smith, for example.

Lesson 8 Student's Book p. 49

Warm-up
Students review facts from the previous page.
- Organize students into teams and carry out a quick-fire quiz about the 2004 Indian Ocean tsunami and about the story of Tilly Smith. Ask, for example, *In which month did the tsunami occur?* (December), *How big was the earthquake that caused the tsunami?* (9.1 – 9.3), *How old was Tilly Smith at the time of the tsunami?* (10 years old).

4 🎧¹⁴ **Rewrite the false statements so that they are correct. Then listen again to check.**

Students correct and rewrite false statements.
- Draw students' attention to the **Guess What!** box about Phuket Island. Discuss the information in the box as a whole class. Elicit the names of well-known vacation destinations in the students' own country and ask them how they think these places compare with Phuket Island.

Answers
1. Tilly Smith was on vacation in Phuket Island, in Thailand.
4. A hotel security guard was the first person who believed what Tilly was saying.
5. The hotel security guard warned the tourists and hotel staff on the beach.

5 Why is Tilly Smith's story a remarkable life-changing experience? Discuss with a partner.

Students discuss their reactions to the text.

Stop and Think! Critical Thinking
Are there any policies to help people cope with natural disasters in your country? Do you know what to do in case of a natural disaster?
- Organize students into small groups and have them discuss policies and measures that exist in their country to help people in the event of a natural disaster, such as an earthquake, a landslide, forest fires, volcanic eruptions, etc.
- Ask them how well prepared they feel they would be if a natural disaster occurred. If necessary, write ideas on the board to get them started.
- Invite groups to share their comments with the rest of the class.

> **Extension**
> Students prepare presentations about natural disasters in their own country.
> - Organize students into small groups and ask them to research and prepare short illustrated presentations about notable natural disasters that have occurred in their own country. Invite students to share their work with the rest of the class.

Wrap-up
Students act out demonstration videos about safety drills for natural disasters.
- Organize students into small groups and have them prepare scenes from an instructional video that tells students how to behave and what to do in the event of, for example, a fire or an earthquake.
- If possible, have students record short videos of their work.

➡ **(No homework today.)**

 **Project**

Objective
Students will be able to create a vlog.

Lesson 9   Student's Book p. 50

Warm-up
Students brainstorm examples of blended expressions (also known as portmanteau words).
- Write a few blended expressions on the board and ask students to separate them into their two parts, for example, *Spanglish* (Spanish + English), *brunch* (breakfast + lunch), *infomercial* (information + commercial), *wiktionary* (wiki + dictionary), *multiplex* (multiple + complex).
- Then ask students to brainstorm more examples of blended or portmanteau expressions.

 52

1 How much do you know about vlogs? Use the words below to talk about them with a classmate.
Students discuss what they know about vlogs.

2 Read the definition. Is there any new information about it that you didn't know?
Students check their ideas against a dictionary definition.

3 Are there any vlogs you often follow or you would like to follow? Complete the chart below.
Students complete a chart about vlogs that they follow.

Answers
Answers will vary.

4 Work in small groups. Share your ideas in Activity 3.
Students share and compare their information from the previous activity.

Extension
Students compile a Top Ten Vlogs list.
- Invite students to work in small groups compiling a list of their Top Ten recommended vlogs. Have them publish their lists around the school.

Wrap-up
Students give presentations about their favorite vlogs.
- Ask students to work alone preparing a short presentation of their favorite vlog. Invite individual students to present their vlogs, using real-life examples, and to share their opinions and comments.

 Teaching Tip
Visualizing Lessons from the Students' Point of View
Try to visualize and hear in your own head the way a lesson or an activity will work in class before you actually teach it. Imagine how it will come across from the students' point of view.

Lesson 10 Student's Book p. 51

Warm-up
Students view a selection of vlog posts.
- To help students become more familiar with the content and the presentation style of a post on a vlog, and to give them more confidence, share a selection of vlog posts with the class and invite observation and comment.

5 **Work in the same groups of Activity 4. You will create a vlog post. Follow the steps below.**
Students work in their groups creating a vlog post.
- Ask students to read carefully the six steps of the instructions. In particular, draw students' attention to the tips which will help them produce a good quality vlog post.
- Have students work together on the creation of their vlog post. As they work, monitor each group and try to ensure that all members of each group contribute to the overall effort.

6 **Now present your vlog post to your classmates.**
Students present their vlog posts to the rest of the class.
- Invite students to share their vlog posts with their classmates and with students from other groups.

Stop and Think! Critical Thinking
Did you learn something new from your classmates? How can the activities in this section impact your life?
- Organize students into small groups and have them discuss what new things they learned from their classmates and how what they saw on someone else's vlog can influence their lives. (If necessary, write ideas on the board to get them started.)
- Invite groups to share their comments with the rest of the class.

The Digital Touch
To incorporate digital media in the project, suggest one or more of the following:
- Encourage students to use free video editing programs and tools to create their vlog posts and to post these on safe video-sharing sites.
- Alternatively, have students present their posts using PowerPoint or similar slide show presentation programs.
- If possible, allow students to upload their work to the school's website.

Note that students should have the option to do a task on paper or digitally.

Extension
Students write a How To guide for first-time vloggers.
- Invite students to write a short guide or manual offering advice to people who want to try creating a vlog for the first time. Encourage students to share their guides with the rest of the class.

Wrap-up
Students compare vlog posts and vote for their favorites.
- Invite students to vote for their favorites from their classmates' vlog posts. There can be awards in various categories, e.g., most useful content, most interesting presentation style, best design, best editing, best use of graphics and sound, best use of technology, best overall presentation, etc.

➡ **Workbook p. 136, Activity 1 (Review)**

 **Review**

Objective
Students will be able to consolidate their understanding of the vocabulary and grammar learned in the unit.

Lesson 11   Student's Book p. 52

> ✔ Homework Check!
> Workbook p. 136, Activity 1 (Review)
> **Answers**
> **1 Complete the sentences using the present perfect continuous or the present perfect.**
> 1. have written, 2. have been learning, 3. haven't created / have not created, 4. haven't had / have not had

Warm-up
Students unscramble vocabulary items related to life experiences.
- Write on the board a series of phrases with certain words scrambled, for example, *attend cigant* (*acting*) *classes*, and have students unscramble the missing words.

1 Look at some objects that different people put together. What are they going to do? Complete the sentences.
Students complete sentences with key vocabulary phrases.

Answers
1. get a part-time job, 2. write a book, 3. travel abroad alone, 4. develop a computer game, 5. create a vlog, 6. learn a foreign language, 7. build a drone, 8. start a band with friends, 9. attend acting classes

2 What are these people doing? Read the short conversations and find out.
Students read short conversations and identify what the speakers are doing.

Answers
1. building a drone, 2. starting a band with friends.

Wrap-up
Students write and act out conversations like the ones in Activity 2.
- Organize students into pairs and have them write conversations similar to the ones in Activity 2 but about other activities, for example, *getting a part-time job, writing a book, traveling abroad alone, developing a computer game, creating a vlog, learning a foreign language, attending acting classes*. Invite pairs of students to share their conversations with the rest of the class.

 (No homework today.)

> **Teaching Tip**
> **Reflecting on Learning**
> As you come to the end of a unit, invite students to reflect on what they enjoyed or did not enjoy so much in the material, what they found easy, difficult, interesting, etc. Most importantly, ask them to identify specific things that they need to work more on so that they can progress.

Lesson 12 Student's Book p. 53

Warm-up

Students review the present perfect and the present perfect continuous.
- Write on the board a series of sentences, some in the present perfect and some in the present perfect continuous, and ask students to convert one form into the other.

3 Complete the sentences with the present perfect continuous.

Students complete sentences using the present perfect continuous.

Answers

1. has been looking, 2. has been helping, 3. Have you been waiting, 4. haven't been attending / have not been attending, 5. has been writing

4 Circle the correct word.

Students complete present perfect continuous sentences with *for* or *since*.

Answers

1. since, 2. since, 3. for

5 Decide if the sentences are Right (R) or Wrong (W). Correct the wrong sentences.

Students check sentences for grammatical accuracy and then correct any incorrect sentences.

Answers

1. W, *has been getting* Lukas has gotten a part-time job as a waiter in a café. 2. W, *haven't been starting* Kyle and Elijah haven't started a band yet. 3. R, 4. R, 5. R

6 Mark (✓) the correct sentence for each picture.

Students look at photos and identify the correct sentences to accompany them.

Answers

1. Kaylee has been packing… 2. My father has written a book… 3. Anna has been flying her drone…

Extension

Students role-play interviews with made-up celebrities.
- Organize students into pairs and have them role-play conversations in which a reporter interviews a famous singer, athlete, actor, politician, etc. Encourage students to use the present perfect in its simple and continuous forms, for example, *How long have you been in a band?*, *Have you been writing any songs recently?* Invite students to share their role plays with the rest of the class.

Big Question

Students are given the opportunity to revisit the Big Question and reflect on it.
Ask students to turn to the unit opener on page 41 and to look at the photo. Elicit observation and comment about the image of the boy at two stages in his life.
Explore the idea that as the boy has changed physically, he has also experienced different things as he grows up.

⭐ Scorecard

Hand out (and/or project) a *Scorecard*. Have students fill in their *Scorecards* for this unit.

➔ **Study for the unit test.**

4 How green do you want to be?

Grammar	Vocabulary
First Conditional vs. Second Conditional: <u>If you ride</u> your bike to school every day, <u>you will save</u> over 167 liters of gas every year. <u>If people stopped</u> using plastic bags, <u>plastic trash would drop</u> dramatically.	**Sustainable Living:** car pool, food leftovers, indoor garden, natural cleaning products (baking soda, vinegar), rechargeable batteries, reusable shopping bags

Listening	Writing
Identifying opinions and facts	Writing a report on a green initiative

How green do you want to be?

In the first lesson, read the unit title aloud and have students look carefully at the unit cover. Encourage them to think about the message in the picture. At the end of the unit, students will discuss the big question: *How green do you want to be?*

 Teaching Tip

Calculating Lesson Times

Many teachers plan their classes by allocating their lesson time forward from the beginning of the lesson (Activity 1: 10 minutes, Activity 2: 15 minutes, etc.). A more effective method is to plan your time in reverse from the end of the lesson, because often the most important work occurs in the key final stages rather than in the lead-ins and warm-ups. Calculate how long it might take your learners to do the final activity, and calculate back to the preceding stage. Calculate the time for that stage, and then the stage before it, and so on.

 Vocabulary

Objective
Students will be able to use **sustainable living** vocabulary to talk about going green.

Lesson 1   Student's Book pp. 56 and 57

Warm-up
Students brainstorm color associations.
- Organize students into pairs or threes and have them brainstorm things, ideas and concepts that are associated with certain colors, for example, *white = purity*. Have students share their ideas as a whole group.

1 Look at the pictures. What do you know about the products or actions shown below?
Students activate knowledge about sustainable living by identifying vocabulary items.
- Ask students to look at the photos. Have students talk in pairs about the products or the actions shown in the pictures. Discuss their ideas as a whole class.

2 Read and complete the texts with the words in Activity 1.
Students complete texts with sustainable living vocabulary items.
- Ask students to look at the texts. Elicit that the texts are leaflets that contain information about how to "go green."
- Have students work alone or in pairs completing the texts with the correct phrases from Activity 1. Check answers.

Answers
White vinegar, baking soda, indoor garden, food leftovers, electric bike, car pool, reusable shopping bags, rechargeable batteries

> **Extension**
> Students prepare scripts for public service announcements about going green.
> - Organize students into small groups and have them use the information in the leaflets on these pages to prepare public service announcements offering advice about how people can go green.

Wrap-up
Students create green-themed crosswords.
- Invite students to work in pairs making crosswords using vocabulary related to sustainable living, for example, *indoor garden, electric bike, car pool, rechargeable batteries*, etc.

➡ **Workbook p. 138, Activities 1 and 2**

 Teaching Tip
Displaying Students' Work
Teenage students are usually pleased to have their work displayed for the rest of the class, or the rest of the school, to see. This may be particularly motivating for those students who have fewer opportunities to have their achievements recognized in terms of more academic measures such as formal tests and evaluations.

Lesson 2 Student's Book p. 57

> ✔ **Homework Check!**
> Workbook p. 138, Activities 1 and 2
> **Answers**
> **1 Complete the sentences using the words below.**
> 1. indoor garden, 2. car pool, 3. white vinegar, baking soda, 4. reusable shopping bags, 5. electric bike, 6. food leftovers
> **2 Which sentence from Activity 1 do these pictures refer to? Number them.**
> *left to right, top to bottom* 2, 6, 3, 4, 5, 0, 1

Warm-up
Students review sustainable living vocabulary items.
- Write on the board the first word of a phrase from Activity 1, for example, *indoor*, and have students give the word that completes it (*garden*). Repeat with other expressions.

3 🎧15 **Listen to people talking about the green actions in the texts. Mark (✓) the actions they mention.**
Students listen for key topic words and phrases.
- Ask students to look at the chart. Elicit the complete phrase for each column heading. Then have students listen and mark the actions that each pair of people mentions. Check answers.

Answers

1. Carry a reusable shopping bag, 2. Ride an electric bike, 3. Grow an indoor garden, 4. Organize a car pool

Audio Script
1
HAILEY: Hey, we don't need the plastic bags!
SYDNEY: Oh, really? How are we going to take the groceries home, then?
HAILEY: Look! I have this beautiful, foldable and fancy shopping bag!
SYDNEY: Wow! It *is* beautiful indeed! And eco-friendly!
2
ABBIE: How did you get here so fast? Did your mom bring you?
TYLER: No! Now I have my own quick and eco-friendly means of transportation. Come outside and look!
ABBIE: A bike?
TYLER: It's not an ordinary bike. It's electric! By the way, is there an outlet around here? I need to recharge it.
3
ANNA: Umm… This spaghetti tastes delicious! What's your secret, Brian?
BRIAN: I made the sauce with tomatoes and basil I grew myself!
ANNA: Really? But how?
BRIAN: Just look at the window, Anna. That's my garden.

ANNA: So you're a cook *and* a gardener. You're definitely a friend with multiple talents!
4
MEGAN: So, is your dad going to bring us tonight, Ben?
BEN: Yes, he is. He's going to go to Justin's and Grace's houses first. You'll be last.
MEGAN: No problem. And my mom will pick us up at the end of the concert.
BEN: Deal!

4 Rank the green attitudes in this section.
Students rank activities according to how green they think they are.
- Ask students to write the eight activities on these pages in order, the greenest being the activity that produces the greatest benefit for the environment.

Answers
Answers will vary.

5 Work with a partner. Answer the questions below.
Students discuss going green.
- Have students answer the questions in pairs. Then discuss the questions with the whole group.

Answers
Answers will vary.

- Draw students' attention to the **Guess What!** box. Read the information aloud and elicit observation and comment.

Wrap-up
Students role-play conversations about going green.
- Organize students into pairs and have them role-play conversations like the ones in Activity 3 but using the following activities: use baking soda for washing laundry, use rechargeable batteries, keep and eat food leftovers, use white vinegar for cleaning.

➡ **Workbook pp. 138 and 139, Activities 3 and 4**

Grammar

Objective
Students will be able to use **the first and second conditionals** to talk about actions that help save the environment.

Lesson 3 — Student's Book p. 58

✔ **Homework Check!**
Workbook pp. 138 and 139, Activities 3 and 4

Answers
3 Cross out the word that doesn't belong. Explain why it's different.
1. ~~baking soda~~, Both car pools and electric bikes are related to transportation. 2. ~~indoor garden~~, Both white vinegar and baking soda are used to clean. 3. ~~reusable shopping bags~~, Both indoor garden and food leftovers produce more food for people.
4 Match the sentences.
1. f, 2. b, 3. e, 4. a, 5. g, 6. d, 7. h

Warm-up
Students play Hangman to review **sustainable living** vocabulary.
- Play Hangman in teams to practice expressions from the previous pages.

1 Read about actions that help save the environment. Mark (✓) the one that depends on an individual attitude.
Students read a text for the general idea.
- Ask students to skim through the article and mark the action that depends on how one individual person acts. Check the answer.

Answers
How much gas will I save if I ride my bike to school every day?

2 Read the article again. Then circle the correct answer.
Students read to understand a language point.
- Ask students to reread the article, more carefully this time, and to think about the meaning of the actions mentioned in bold type in the article. Have students read the questions and circle the correct options. Check answers.

Answers
1. Action 2, 2. Action 1

- Draw students' attention to the box with information about the *First Conditional* and the *Second Conditional* and clarify any doubts that students may have about form or meaning.

3 Use the code below to identify the structures in Activity 1.
Students identify key parts of the form of conditional sentences.
- Ask students to identify the different parts that make up the structure of the conditional sentences in the article.

Answers
Circle If you live…, if you get to school…
Highlight in yellow you will save over 167 liters…, you will save 395 kg…, you will certainly become fit…, your mom and dad will be happy…, they won't have to worry…
Underline if people stopped using… if we replaced shopping plastic bags…
Highlight in green plastic trash would drop…, one supermarket chain in the United States wouldn't need to buy…, tons of resources would be saved…

Extension
Students make Going Green posters.
- Organize students into groups and invite them to create Going Green posters for their school, focusing on actions that students themselves can take to improve the environment. Display students' work around the classroom.

Wrap-up
Students play a game using conditionals.
- Organize students into teams. Write on the board the first half of a conditional sentence (first or second conditional), for example, *If you used rechargeable batteries…* and challenge students to think of as many ways as they can to finish the sentence logically. Award points for the most original answers.

➡ **Workbook p. 139, Activity 1**

 Teaching Tip
Giving Students Time to Think
During class, be sure to give students enough time to listen, think and process their thoughts so that they can then ask or answer a question. While giving them time to think, resist the temptation to talk!

Lesson 4 — Student's Book p. 59

> ✔ **Homework Check!**
> Workbook p. 139, Activity 1
> **Answers**
> **1 Read and circle the correct verb.**
> 1. would, 2. would, 3. would, 4. will, 5. would,
> 6. will, 7. will, 8. would

Warm-up

Students complete sentences with the correct verb forms.
- Write on the board a series of conditional sentences, some first conditional and some second conditional. Leave blanks in place of the words *will*, *won't*, *would* or *wouldn't* in the result clauses of the sentences. Ask students to supply the correct verb form to complete each sentence.

4 Match the sentence halves.

Students match the two halves (conditions and results) of conditional sentences.
- Read aloud the first sentence half and elicit the correct way to finish it (*I will use it to go to school every day.*). Then have students work alone or in pairs matching the rest of the sentence halves. Check answers.

Answers

If my dad gives me an electric bike for Christmas, I will use it to go to school every day. Would you use vinegar and baking soda if you had to clean the whole house? If Eric's mom didn't organize the car pool, I would have to walk to school three times a week. My family and the neighbors will start a community garden if we get permission from the City Council to use an abandoned area near my house. Will you eat the leftovers from yesterday's dinner if I make a nice salad to go with them? Danny wouldn't recycle the shopping bags if we didn't convince him to do it.

5 Complete the conversations. Use the first or second conditionals.

Students complete conversations with the correct conditional forms.
- Ask students to work alone or in pairs completing each sentence with the correct conditional form (first or second) of the given verb. Check answers.

Answers

1. don't, won't ride, 2. were, wouldn't end up, 3. Will, help, gives, 4. Would, continue

6 Now number the pictures according to the conversations in Activity 5 they refer to.

Students match photos with texts.
- Ask students to look at the photos. Have them label each photo with the correct number of the conversation in Activity 5. Check answers.

Answers

left to right 4, 3, 1, 2

7 Think Fast! Complete the sentences using your own ideas.

Students do a two-minute timed challenge: completing conditional statements.
- Ask students to read and complete the conditional statements with their own ideas. Compare and discuss answers as a whole class.

Answers

Answers will vary.

Wrap-up

Students compile quizzes about ethical questions.
- Organize students into teams. Invite them to compile multiple-choice questions about ethical situations, for example, *If you found a large sum of money in the street, would you…* a) *hand it in to the police,* b) *keep it for yourself,* c) *give it to charity.*

▶ **Workbook p. 140, Activities 2 and 3**

> 🐝 **Teaching Tip**
> **Keeping Track of Your Class Time**
> To better understand where your class time really goes, keep a log for a few days noting how long you and your class take to accomplish certain everyday tasks. Once you have identified activities that rob you of valuable time, create a more efficient way of working.

 **Listening & Writing**

Objectives
Students will be able to identify **opinions** and **facts** and **write a report** on a green initiative.

Lesson 5 — Student's Book p. 60

✔ **Homework Check!**
Workbook p. 140, Activities 2 and 3
Answers
2 Complete the sentences.
1. will, 2. would, 3. will, 4. would, 5. will
3 Complete the sentences by writing the result clause.
Answers will vary.

Warm-up

 62

Students unscramble conditional sentences.
- Write on the board some short conditional sentences and have students write them in the correct order.

1 Read the biodata of Ellen Parker, who was interviewed for a podcast. What do you think she will talk about?
Students read a person's biodata to make predictions about a podcast.
- Ask students to look at the photo and to read the biodata. Ask them to say what they think Dr. Parker's podcast will be about. Discuss answers.

2 🎧¹⁶ Now listen to the interview. Check your predictions in Activity 1.
Students listen to check their predictions.
- Have students listen to the interview to check their ideas about the podcast.

Audio Script
INTERVIEWER: Thank you very much for joining us today, Dr. Parker.
ELLEN: My pleasure.
INTERVIEWER: So, climate change is a reality, but there are people who still don't believe it. What do you have to say to these people?
ELLEN: I think these people are afraid of facing climate change. We have seen the effects, we also have scientific evidence of climate change and we can't deny this evidence. If we don't act fast, we will have serious problems in the future.
INTERVIEWER: And what are some of these effects?
ELLEN: Well, there are many, and most of them are related to each other. I'd like to point out two main effects. The first is: the level of the sea is rising. According to NASA satellites, it rose 17 centimeters in the 20th century. If the sea level continues to rise, some islands like the Maldives, in the Indian Ocean, will disappear.
INTERVIEWER: That sounds terrible!

ELLEN: It is terrible indeed! And unfortunately, that is not the only effect. The second effect is that it is clear that the planet is getting warmer. Meteorologic registers show that the global temperature has been rising since 1880 and that this warming has become much more intense since the 1970s. Just to give you an idea of how serious this is, according to the American Meteorologist Society, the ten warmest years have all happened between 1998 and 2014! If the average temperature around the globe increases by 2 degrees, hurricanes, for example, will get stronger and much more destructive. I believe that governments must take action to stop global warming, and they must do it now!

- Draw students' attention to the **Be Strategic!** box and ask them to read the information. Remind students of the difference between opinions and facts.

3 🎧¹⁶ Listen to the interview again. Complete the summary with the words from the box.
Students listen and complete a summary.
- Ask students to listen to the interview again and to complete the summary with the correct words. Check answers.

Answers
1. NASA, 2. 17, 3. 20th, 4. islands, 5. 1880,
6. 1970, 7. The American Meteorologist Society,
8. hurricanes, 9. stronger, 10. destructive

Wrap-up

Students listen to an altered audio script and spot differences.
- Read aloud the audio script but with a number of key differences. Ask students to identify the places where you deviated from the script.

➡ **Workbook p. 141, Activity 1**

Lesson 6 — Student's Book pp. 60 and 61

✔ **Homework Check!**
Workbook p. 141, Activity 1

Answers
1 Read the title. Mark (✓) the ideas you think the text will mention. Then read and check.
a, b, d

Warm-up
Students role-play questions and answers for a radio call-in show.
- Organize students into small groups and invite them to role-play conversations in which people call in to a radio show to ask questions of "experts." Encourage students to use, *If I were you…* in their answers.

4 🎧16 **Listen to the interview once more. Label the items in the interview according to the code below.**
Students listen to identify opinions, facts and supporting evidence.
- Ask students to listen one more time and to label the items in the interview according to whether they are opinions, facts or pieces of evidence that support a fact. Check answers.

Answers
1. O, 2. F, 3. SE, 4. O, 5. F, 6. SE, 7. SE, 8. O

5 **Now read this report about a green initiative in a high school. Then answer the questions below in your notebook.**
Students read a report and answer comprehension questions.
- Read aloud the title of the report. Check that students understand the word *initiative* (a strategy intended to resolve a difficulty or improve a situation). Then have them read the report and answers.

Answers
1. to start a community garden, 2. to grow healthy vegetables and herbs to be used in the school kitchen, 3. money and training, 4. Answers will vary.

6 **Think Fast!** Can you label four of the vegetables and herbs below in your language and in English? They are all mentioned in the report!
Students do a thirty-second timed challenge: labeling vegetables and herbs.
- Ask students to work in pairs labeling the four food items in their first language and in English. Check answers.

Answers
left to right chives, tomatoes, parsley, lettuce

7 **Now you are going to research and write a report on a green initiative in your country or around the world. Use the chart to outline your report in your notebook.**
Students carry out research for a report about a green initiative.
- Read aloud the chart headings, then ask students to work in pairs researching information about a green initiative. Encourage them to use the chart to organize their information.

Answers
Answers will vary.

8 **Now write your report in your notebook. Then present it to the class.**
Students write their reports from Activity 7.
- Ask students to write out their final reports using the information they researched in the previous activity. Invite students to share their reports with the rest of the class.

Wrap-up
Students make sentences using key vocabulary items.
- As a quick-fire game, give students key vocabulary items from these pages (*climate change, sea level, temperature, organic gardening,* etc.) and from the **Glossary** (*evidence, soil*) and ask them to come up with a sentence containing that item.

➡ **Workbook p. 141, Activity 2**

Preparing for the Next Lesson
Ask students to watch an introduction to green initiatives in Sweden: http://goo.gl/HjOfZj
or invite them to consult the following website:
http://goo.gl/7aeUcI

# Culture

Objectives
Students will be able to talk about Sweden, the greenest country in the world.

Lesson 7 — Student's Book pp. 62 and 63

> ✔ **Homework Check!**
> Workbook p. 141, Activity 2
> **Answers**
> **2 In your notebook, fill in a chart with challenges to going green and solutions.**
> Answers will vary.

Warm-up

Students identify the countries of Scandinavia and also other Nordic countries.
- Provide students with a plain map of the region (with borders but without country names) and ask them to try to label the map with the names *Denmark*, *Norway* and *Sweden*.
- Elicit or explain that these three countries comprise Scandinavia, and that other Nordic countries like Finland and Iceland are often also included under this grouping.

1 What do you know about Sweden? Circle the options in the chart. The pictures in the brochure will help you.
Students access existing knowledge and/or make deductions about a topic.
- Ask students to look at the brochure and the photos. Have them use the pictures and their existing knowledge to circle the best options in the chart. Check answers.

Answers
left to right Stockholm, Temperate/Subarctic, Gamla Stan and Drottningholm Palace, Answers will vary.

- Draw students' attention to the *Guess What!* box. Read the information aloud and elicit observation and comment. Ask students if they know the population density of their own country.

2 Read the text about some green initiatives in Sweden. Then write YES or NO for the statements below.
Students read a text and then mark statements as true or false.
- Ask students to read the text carefully and then to read the statements and to mark each one *Yes* or *No* accordingly. Check answers. Then have students correct the false statements with the correct information.

Answers
1. YES, 2. NO (The city plants the roof gardens.), 3. NO (The city government also invests in solar panels and recycling.), 4. NO (Community and indoor gardens have been popular for a long time.), 5. YES, 6. YES

> ### Extension
> Students create Compare and Contrast posters.
> - Organize students into small groups and invite them to create information posters comparing and contrasting Sweden with their own country. They can consider aspects such as: population, area, language(s), type of government, capital city, currency, etc.
> - Have students display their work around the class.

Wrap-up
Students play a guessing game about places in Sweden.
- Organize students into two teams. A player from one team imagines being in a certain place in Sweden (taken from the information on these pages) and describes what he or she is doing, giving gradual clues as to the location. Players from the other team try to guess where the player is.

 (No homework today.)

> ### 🐝 Teaching Tip
> **Playing Background Music in Class**
> While students are working quietly alone, try playing some soft, soothing classical music in the background. Alternatively, try playing music mixed with sounds from nature (rivers, rain forests, etc.).

Lesson 8 Student's Book p. 63

Warm-up
Students recap information from the previous lesson.
- With books closed, give students key place names from the brochure on page 62 and the webpage on page 63, for example, Gamla Stan, and ask students to recall everything they can remember about that place.

3 ¹⁷ **Listen to two conversations. Mark (✓) the green initiative they are talking about.**

Students listen to two short conversations and identify the topic of each one.
- Ask students to look at the chart. Then have them listen to the conversations and mark the green initiative that is the topic of each conversation. Check answers. As extension, ask students to practice the conversations in pairs.

Answers
Conversation 1. Urban Farming,
Conversation 2. Vintage Clothing

Audio Script
1
TEEN GIRL 1: And what do you grow here?
TEEN BOY: We grow all kinds of vegetables: tomatoes, potatoes, lettuce, kale, herbs… and they are all organic!
TEEN GIRL 1: That's amazing!
2
TEEN GIRL 2: What beautiful jeans!
TEEN GIRL 3: Yeah, they're from the 90s and are made of organic cotton!
TEEN GIRL 2: Cool!

Stop and Think! Value
Which of the initiatives in Activity 2 could be taken in your city or country? Why?
- Organize students into small groups and have them discuss which of the initiatives mentioned in Activity 2 could be taken up in the students' own country. (If necessary, write ideas on the board to get them started.)
- Invite groups to share their comments with the rest of the class.

> **Extension**
> Students prepare travel brochures.
> - Organize students into small groups and invite them to prepare travel brochures like the one on page 62 about their own country or about another country of their choice. Display students' work around the classroom.

Wrap-up
Students role-play street interviews.
- Organize students into pairs and have them role-play conversations in which one student is a radio reporter and other student is a) a resident of Augustenborg who looks after some of the green roofs of the town, or b) a person who grows vegetables in an urban garden or c) a second-hand clothes seller in Vintagemassan.

▶ **(No homework today.)**

 **Project**

Objectives
Students will be able to create an action plan to implement a green initiative at school.

Lesson 9 Student's Book pp. 64 and 65

Warm-up
Students brainstorm ideas about the color green.
- Organize students into small groups and have them brainstorm a list of associations about the color green. Encourage them to go into more detail beyond the more obvious connections with nature, trees, leaves, etc. and to consider emotional states (calm, safety) or more abstract concepts (freshness, harmony). Discuss students' ideas as a whole class.

1 **How green is your school? Look at the quiz about eco-friendly attitudes and mark (✓) the ones your school already adopts. Then read the results.**
Students read a survey quiz and identify actions that their school has adopted.
- Ask students to look at the quiz. Elicit observation and comment about the design and layout of the survey (the coloring, the style of the lettering, the illustrations, etc.)
- Have students work in pairs answering the quiz by marking the actions that their school has already adopted. Check and discuss the results as a whole class. Invite students to share their reactions to the results.

Answers
Answers will vary.

2 **Work in small groups. Based on the result above, choose a green initiative you would like to implement in your school. You can even use one of the actions in the quiz.**
Students select a green initiative to work on for their project.
- Organize students into small groups and ask them to choose a green initiative that they would like to adopt in their school.

3 **Now brainstorm ideas for an action plan to implement your initiative. Look at the example below.**
Students study an example of an action plan.
- Ask students to look closely at the example. Make sure that students understand the column headings. Stress the importance of delegating specific individuals to carry out certain tasks and the importance of setting "begin" and "end" dates to ensure that the project stays on schedule.

Wrap-up
Students comment on the example of an action plan in Activity 3.
- Organize students into small groups and ask them to comment on the action plan, making suggestions for any changes that they would make if this were their plan.

🌩 Teaching Tip
Estimating Lesson Timing
As a general rule, it is probably better to overplan a little for a lesson and to not get around to doing the final activity than to get to the end of a lesson and be short of things to do. Most likely, unused materials or activities can be recycled or repurposed in a subsequent lesson.

Lesson 10   Student's Book p. 65

Warm-up
Students answer questions about Earth Day.
- As a whole class, do a quick-fire quiz to see what students know about Earth Day. Ask *When is Earth Day celebrated?* (April 22), *In what year was it first celebrated?* (1970), *In how many countries is it now celebrated?* (193).

4 Write your own plan on a separate sheet of paper. Follow the steps below.
Students work in their groups creating an action plan.
- Have students read through the steps carefully, then organize them into groups and ask them to write their own plan for a green initiative, dividing the goal into tasks and key activities, discussing who will be responsible for each task and setting realistic begin and end dates.

5 Now present your action plan to the class.
Students present their action plans.
- Invite students to share their action plans with the rest of the class.

Stop and Think! Critical Thinking
Which action plan would have more of a chance to be implemented in your school? Why?
- Organize students into small groups and have them discuss which of the groups' action plans they think would have more of a chance of being adopted in their school. Regarding the action plans that students feel would not be implemented, invite them to suggest why this might be. (If necessary, write ideas on the board to get them started.)
- Invite groups to share their comments with the rest of the class.

The Digital Touch
To incorporate digital media in the project, suggest one or more of the following:
- Invite students to present their action plans using PowerPoint or similar slide show presentation programs.
- If possible, allow students to upload their work to the school's website.

Note that students should have the option to do a task on paper or digitally.

Extension
Students research "green" political parties.
- Organize students into small groups and invite them to research "green" parties in their own country or in other countries and to find out about their policies and their achievements. Invite students to share their findings with the rest of the class.

Wrap-up
Students compare action plans and vote for their favorites.
- Invite students to vote for their favorites from their classmates' action plans. There can be commendations in various categories, e.g., the most practical plan, the most beneficial plan, the most original presentation style, the best use of graphics and images, the best overall presentation, etc.

➡ **Workbook p. 140, Activity 1 (Review)**

Review

Objective
Students will be able to consolidate their understanding of the vocabulary and grammar learned in the unit.

Lesson 11 Student's Book p. 66

✔ **Homework Check!**
Workbook p. 140, Activity 1 (Review)
Answers
1 Write about five changes you plan to make to help the environment and the result of those changes. Use the first conditional.
Answers will vary.

Warm-up
Students make an Environment Alphabet.
- Organize students into small groups and challenge them to come up with an environment-related word beginning with each letter of the alphabet, for example, *atmosphere*, *biodegradable*, *climate*, etc.

1 Complete the crossword puzzle. Use the sentence hints to help you.
Students complete a crossword puzzle.
- Read aloud the first Down clue and elicit the correct answer (*baking*). Then have students work alone or in pairs completing the rest of the crossword puzzle. Check answers.

Answers
1. baking, 2. leftovers, 3. electric, 4. pool,
5. batteries, 6. vinegar, 7. shopping, 8. garden

2 What is wrong with these conversations? Correct them.
Students find errors in conversations and correct them.
- With the help of a student, read aloud the first conversation and elicit the two-word phrase that is incorrect (*reusable bike*) and the correct expression (*electric bike*). Then have students work alone or in pairs completing the rest of the exercise. Check answers.

Answers
1. ~~reusable~~ electric, 2. ~~an electric~~ a car,
3. ~~rechargeable~~ reusable, 4. ~~white~~ baking

Wrap-up
Students create their own word puzzles.
- Organize students into pairs and invite them to create their own crossword puzzles (or other word puzzles such as wordsearches) using vocabulary items from this unit. Encourage students to make copies of their puzzles to share with their classmates.

▶ **(No homework today.)**

 Teaching Tip
Using Flexible Lesson Plans
Try writing your lesson plan ideas on sticky notes (such as Post-it notes) so that if things do not go exactly as planned, you can quickly move things around into a new sequence.

Lesson 12 Student's Book p. 67

Warm-up

Students identify first and second conditional sentences.

- Write on the board a series of conditional sentences, some first conditional and some second conditional. Simply ask students to say which is which.

3 Complete the short conversations. Use the first conditional.

Students complete conversations with the correct verb forms.

- Ask students to look at the first item. Elicit the correct answers for the first three spaces (*will, do, removes*). Then have students work alone or in pairs completing the rest of the conversations with the correct first conditional verb forms. Check answers.

Answers

1. will, do, removes, will, put, take, 2. plug, will, take, 3. move, will build, will, visit, does, 4. don't start, won't be able, won't have, continue

4 Write sentences from the prompts in your notebook. Use the second conditional.

Students write sentences from cues.

- Ask students to look at the first item. Elicit the correct second conditional sentence from the prompts. (*If I became a millionaire, I would donate some money to protect the rainforest.*) Then have students work alone or in pairs writing out the rest of the sentences with the correct second conditional verb forms. Check answers.

Answers

1. If I became a millionaire, I would donate some money to protect the rainforest. 2. If we stopped drinking bottled water, tons of plastic would be saved. 3. If Americans replaced one regular light bulb with a fluorescent bulb, the pollution reduction would be the same as removing one million cars from the streets. 4. If people didn't pre-heat their ovens when cooking, they would pay less on their gas or electricity bills. 5. If my mom was allowed to work from home, she would spend less time in traffic and save gas.

5 Rewrite the sentences below. Use the first or the second conditional.

Students rewrite sentences using conditional forms.

- Read aloud the first item and ask students to say if it refers to a real, possible situation or an unreal situation. Then elicit a second conditional sentence to express the same situation another way. (*If we had an area with soil in the schoolyard, we would grow a community garden in our school.*) Have students work alone or in pairs completing the rest of the activity. Check answers.

Answers

1. If we had an area with soil in the schoolyard, we would grow a community garden in our school. 2. If I have time, I will attend the gardening workshop on the weekend. 3. If her co-workers didn't live far from our house, my mom would organize a car pool to work. 4. If my sister doesn't make a soup with the chicken leftovers, I will make a sandwich with them when I get home.

❓ Big Question

Students are given the opportunity to revisit the Big Question and reflect on it.

- Ask students to turn to the unit opener on page 55 and to look at the illustration. Elicit observation and comment about the stylized image of the Earth as a very green place.
- Read aloud the question and, with the whole group, discuss to what extent it is up to us how green the planet can be. Or, in other words, if human activity has caused so many environmental problems, what can the human race now do to reverse the damage?

⭐ Scorecard

Hand out (and/or project) a *Scorecard*. Have students fill in their *Scorecards* for this unit.

➡ **Study for the unit test.**

5 Is reality stranger than fiction?

Grammar
Modals of Speculation – Past: Aliens **must / might / could have** built the statues on the island.

Vocabulary
Supernatural Things, Creatures and Phenomena: alien, clairvoyance, ghost, telekinesis, telepathy, UFO, werewolf, zombie

Reading
Identifying and organizing key information

Writing
Writing an explanation using modal verbs

Is reality stranger than fiction?

In the first lesson, read the unit title aloud and have students look carefully at the unit cover. Encourage them to think about the message in the picture. At the end of the unit, students will discuss the big question: *Is reality stranger than fiction?*

Teaching Tip
Correcting Mistakes Anonymously
Make notes of students' mistakes as you monitor their work, then write them on the board and give the students themselves the opportunity to correct them in pairs or small groups. If nobody knows the right answer, do tell them, but only as a last resort. Anonymous error correction is a gentle way to deal with mistakes. It is not important who made the original mistake; the point is, can the students all correct it? It is a good idea to modify the mistakes that you write on the board so that even the perpetrators do not recognize them as their own. For example, if the original error was, *I have been to the theater last week.* write on the board, *I have been to the movies last week* and correct the mistake: *I went…*

 Vocabulary

Objective
Students will be able to use **supernatural things, creatures and phenomena** vocabulary to talk about strange occurrences.

Lesson 1   Student's Book pp. 70 and 71

Warm-up
Students discuss movie titles.
- Write on the board the names of old movies that deal with supernatural creatures, extraterrestrials, etc. (*Invasion of the Bodysnatchers, Bride of Frankenstein, The Incredible Shrinking Man, Planet of the Vampires*, etc.) Leave gaps in the titles and ask students to guess the missing words.

1 Five pictures are missing from the article. Read it and then number the images on the right as they should be placed in the text.
Students match images with texts.
- Ask students to look at the website. Elicit ideas about what the photos have in common. Have them read the article and match the images on the right with the correct texts by writing the number of each text next to the corresponding image.

Answers
top to bottom 2, 7, 3, 8, 5

2 Organize the phenomena, things and creatures in Activity 1 in the chart below.
Students sort items from Activity 1 into categories.
- Ask students to look at the chart. Check that they know what the headings refer to, respectively: the supposed ability to perceive things using means other than the known senses, hypothetical or fictional beings from outer space, creatures that can only be explained by forces beyond scientific understanding or the laws of nature.
- Have students complete the chart with the items from Activity 1. Check answers.

Answers
Extrasensory Perception (ESP) telepathy, clairvoyance, telekinesis, *Extraterrestrial* aliens, UFOs, *Supernatural Creatures*, zombies, ghosts, werewolves

- Draw students' attention to the **Guess What!** box. Read the information aloud and ask students if they have heard of this famous incident. Elicit observation and comment.

Extension
Students present information about local examples of strange supernatural or paranormal phenomena.
- Organize students into groups and invite them to research and present information about reports or legends of supernatural creatures, sightings of extraterrestrials, etc. in their own country or region.

Wrap-up
Students invent their own titles for movies.
- Refer students back to the warm-up and invite them to work in pairs inventing original and amusing titles for movies about extraterrestrials, extrasensory perception, supernatural creatures, etc.

 Workbook p. 142, Activities 1 and 2

Teaching Tip
Using a Kitchen Timer
A kitchen timer is an invaluable tool for the classroom. You can use it for marking transitions, for signaling the end of group discussion time, cleanup time, etc.

Lesson 2 Student's Book p. 71

> ✔ **Homework Check!**
> Workbook p. 142, Activities 1 and 2
>
> **Answers**
> **1 Label the pictures.**
> *left to right, first row* zombies, werewolf
> *second row* telekinesis, ghost, alien
> **2 Read and match the word with its definition.**
> *top to bottom* clairvoyance, telepathy, UFO, werewolf, telekinesis, *alien*, zombie, ghost

Warm-up

Students practice **supernatural things, creatures, and phenomena** vocabulary with scrambled words.
- Write on the board a series of vocabulary items from the previous page but with the letters scrambled, for example, *revoswelew* (werewolves), *hyleptate* (telepathy) and have students unscramble them.

3 🎧¹⁸ **Listen to a scientist providing explanations for three of the items in Activity 1. Number the creatures and phenomena she talks about.**
Students listen and identify the topics of a scientist's explanations.
- Ask students to listen to the scientist and to identify the three phenomena that she talks about and to number them in the order they are mentioned. Check answers.

Answers

1. Telekinesis, 2. Ghosts, 3. UFO Sightings

Audio Script
1
DR. BAILEY: The great magician Harry Houdini wrote about this "phenomenon" in the beginning of the 20th century. In most cases, hidden wires and other strategies are used to give viewers the impression the object is moving. There is no scientific evidence people can use their minds to interfere with an object.
2
DR. BAILEY: Spirits don't haunt people. Science hasn't been able to prove it. Most apparitions can be credited to hallucinations and even to carbon monoxide poisoning.
3
DR. BAILEY: Alien spaceship sightings can have several explanations. One of them is that meteors commonly enter the Earth's atmosphere and might look like an aircraft in the sky. Weather balloons are also easily mistaken for alien crafts.

4 Answer the questions below.
Students answer questions about their own opinions and ideas regarding supernatural and paranormal phenomena, etc.
- Ask students to work alone answering the questions.

Answers

Answers will vary.

5 Share your ideas in Activity 4 with a partner.
Students compare and discuss their answers from the previous activity.
- Organize students into pairs and ask them to compare and discuss their answers to the questions in the previous activity.
- As extension, arrange students into groups of four and have them discuss their ideas further.
- To end, as a whole-class activity, elicit which of the four questions generated the most discussion.

Stop and Think! Critical Thinking

Why are people so interested in supernatural phenomena?
- Organize students into small groups and have them discuss why they think people are so interested in supernatural or paranormal phenomena. (If necessary, write ideas on the board to get them started.)
- Invite groups to share their comments with the rest of the class.

Wrap-up

Students role-play eyewitness reports of supernatural or paranormal phenomena.
- Organize students into pairs and invite them to role-play conversations in which a TV or radio reporter interviews an eyewitness to a paranormal event, such as telekinesis, or a supernatural creature, such as a werewolf.

➡ **Workbook p. 142, Activity 3**

Grammar

Objective
Students will be able to use **modals of speculation** to talk about unsolved mysteries.

Lesson 3   Student's Book pp. 72 and 73

> ✔ **Homework Check!**
> Workbook p. 142, Activity 3
> **Answers**
> **3 Read and correct the mistake in each sentence. Pay attention to the words in bold.**
> 1. UFO, 2. telepathy, 3. aliens

Warm-up
Students play *Hangman* to review supernatural things, creatures, and phenomena vocabulary.
- Play *Hangman* in teams to practice vocabulary items from the previous page.

1 Read the unsolved mysteries. Then mark (✓) in the chart below which story each possible explanation refers to.
Students read and match mysteries with possible explanations.
- Ask students to look briefly at just the illustrations and elicit ideas regarding what the texts might be about. Then ask students to read the reports and to mark in the chart which of the two stories each explanation refers to. Check answers.

Answers
1. Story #2, 2. Story #1, 3. Story #1, 4. Story #2

- Draw students' attention to the **Guess What!** box. Read the information aloud and elicit observation and comment. Ask students if they know anything about North Korea (established as a separate country from South Korea in 1948, leader Kim Jong-un, etc.).

2 Complete the sentences with the past form of the modals and the verbs in parentheses.
Students complete a text with the correct past forms of modals of speculation.
- Read aloud the beginning of the text up to the first gap and elicit the correct answer (*could have built*), then have students work alone or in pairs completing the rest of the exercise. Check answers.

Answers
1. could have built, 2. might have done, 3. might have been, 4. might not have been, 5. must have been buried

- Draw students' attention to the box with information about **Modals of Speculation in the Past** and clarify any doubts that students may have about form or meaning. Check that students understand the concept of speculation—the forming of a theory without complete evidence or proof.

Extension
Students research and present information about ancient stone structures.
- Organize students into pairs or small groups and invite them to find information about ancient stone structures from any part of the world (for example, pyramids in Egypt, Easter Island statues, etc.) and to give a presentation including speculation about how the structures were built.

Wrap-up
Students speculate about classroom mysteries.
- Organize students into two teams. One team gives an example of a minor mystery that could happen at any school—the more everyday the mystery, the better—for example, the board eraser is missing. The other team has to speculate and offer explanations about what happened, the wilder and more imaginative the explanations, the better.

▶ **Workbook p. 143, Activities 1 and 2**

 **Teaching Tip**
Bringing Nature into the Classroom
If possible, decorate your classroom with indoor garden plants. They make the learning environment more attractive and can have positive effects on students' well-being and performance.

Lesson 4   Student's Book p. 73

> ✔ **Homework Check!**
> Workbook p. 143, Activitiies 1 and 2
> **Answers**
> **1 Read and match the facts with the speculations.**
> *top to bottom* 2, 0, 1, 4, 3
> **2 Look at the pictures and circle the word to complete the sentence.**
> 1. could have, must not have, 2. must not have, could have

Warm-up
Students recall facts from the last lesson.
- Ask questions to see what students can remember about Stonehenge.

3 Use the prompts to speculate about the stories in Activity 1. Use *must (not) have, could / couldn't have,* and *might (not) have*, according to how certain you think each explanation is.
Students use modal verbs to speculate about stories.
- Ask students to read the stories in Activity 1 and, using the prompts, to write explanations. Elicit answers.

Answers
1. Aliens [modal] have abducted the men on the ship. 2. The blobs [modal] have been pieces of jellyfish from an explosion. 3. Aliens [modal] have discarded their experiments over Oakland. 4. North Korea [modal] have sent fishermen to sea with poor equipment.

4 🎧19 Listen to a radio report about a strange phenomenon. Then write sentences in your notebook with possible explanations, according to different people.
Students listen and write sentences.
- Ask students to listen to the recording and write explanations. Elicit answers.

Answers
Answers will vary.

Audio Script
Radio news host: Hundreds of residents of Springville called 911 last night reporting they were seeing strange lights in the sky. According to emergency authorities, people were in a panic and claimed the lights were moving fast, making circular movements with no reasonable explanation. WCKJ talked with one of the distressed citizens. Mrs. Strickland says it all started at about 9 p.m.
Mrs. Strickland: I went outside to look for my cat, Fluffy. He always comes home for dinner, but I couldn't find him anywhere, I think that maybe the lights scared him. Then I looked at the sky—it was a bright, clear night—and saw the lights. They were different colors and moved fast, making circular movements. I was terrified! I strongly believe they were aliens, there's no other possible explanation for them!

Radio news host: WCKJ also got in touch with Fort Spencer Military Base, located 50 kilometers from Springville. They confirmed they were running tests with meteorological balloons last night, and that these balloons had lights on them. According to the military, although the balloons don't fly in circles, this is the most reasonable explanation for the lights. They say the population should not panic and that there's no evidence of any extraterrestrial activity on Earth.
To add more mystery to last night's strange phenomena, astronomers reported unusual meteor activity in the Springville area, which would have caused sightings of shooting stars. But once again, these scientists say that shooting stars simply fall from the sky; they don't keep moving around, as reported by hundreds of people in Springville.
Now to our next story: two people were injured in a car accident…

5 Think Fast! Work with a partner. Can you come up with another explanation for the lights in Springville?
Students do a one-minute timed activity: thinking of alternative explanations.
- Have students work in pairs coming up with their own explanations about the mysterious lights.

Stop and Think! Critical Thinking
What is the best explanation for the unsolved mysteries in Activity 4? Why?
- Have students discuss in small groups which explanation is the best.

Wrap-up
Students vote for their favorite mystery.
- By a quick show-of-hands vote, find out which is the students' favorite mystery.

➡ **Workbook pp. 143 and 144, Activities 3 and 4**

Reading & Writing

Objectives
Students will be able to **identify and organize key information** and **write an explanation using past modal verbs**.

Lesson 5 — Student's Book pp. 74 and 75

> ✔ **Homework Check!**
> Workbook pp. 143 and 144, Activities 3 and 4
>
> **Answers**
> **3 Read and choose the correct meaning of the response.**
> 1. I think you left it in the car. 2. I'm not sure if he was there. 3. I don't believe he won either.
> 4. It's possible that there was an accident.
> **4 Read and rewrite the underlined sentences using modal verbs and keeping the same meaning.**
> Answers will vary.

Warm-up
Students identify true and false statements about a text.
- With books closed, read aloud a series of statements about the mysterious disappearances of Agatha Christie and Amelia Earhart and ask students to say which ones are true and which are false. For example, say, *Agatha Christie disappeared in September, 1926.* (False: December, 1926.)

1 Read these reports of famous disappearances. Underline the most appropriate title for each document.
Students skim texts and match titles with texts.
- Ask students to look at the texts and the photos. Elicit that they have an old-fashioned look (yellowed paper, black and white photos, typewritten text, rubber stamps saying UNSOLVED).
- Have students skim through the texts quickly and then select the best title for each report. Check answers.

Answers
left to right The Mysterious Disappearance of an American Legend, The Most Mysterious Days of a Mystery Writer

2 Compare and contrast Amelia Earhart's and Agatha Christie's stories. Organize your ideas in the diagram, writing at least three things for each item.
Students organize key information from two reports in a Venn diagram.
- Ask students to look at the diagram. Make sure that they understand its three sections. Have them work alone or in pairs sorting and organizing information from the two reports in the diagram in the corresponding sections. Elicit and discuss answers.

Answers
Answers will vary.

Draw students' attention to the **Be Strategic!** box and ask them to read the information. Ask students about other types of information that can be organized using Venn diagrams.

> **Extension**
> Students present information about other mysterious cases of people going missing.
> - Organize students into groups and invite them to research and present information about famous cases of a person going missing in mysterious circumstances.

Wrap-up
Students role-play conversations between the friends or family members of a missing person.
- Organize students into pairs and have them role-play conversations in which friends or family members of Amelia Earhart or Agatha Christie (or some other figure—real-life or invented) talk about their disappearance.

▶ **Workbook p. 145, Activities 1 and 2**

> 💬 **Teaching Tip**
> **Exploiting Cross-Curricular Links**
> Be ready to take advantage of links and overlaps between different areas of the school curricula. Look for ways to bring math, music, social science, art, etc. into the English lesson.

76

Lesson 6
Student's Book p. 75

> ✔ **Homework Check!**
> Workbook p. 145, Activities 1 and 2
> **Answers**
> **1 Read the article. Then complete each definition with an underlined word from the article.**
> 1. genius, 2. recite
> **2 Read and find…**
> 1. reciting numbers from memory, 2. it is not real, 3. children who have difficulty communicating in their native language may be better able to communicate in other ways.

Warm-up
Students test their memory about facts from a text.
- With books closed, read aloud a series of incomplete sentences about the disappearances of Agatha Christie and Amelia Earhart. Ask students to supply the missing information. Say, for example, *Amelia Earhart was the first woman to fly across the _____ Ocean by herself.* (Atlantic)

3 Now read some theories for the disappearances of Amelia Earhart and Agatha Christie. Which do you think is the best? Discuss with your classmates and teacher.
Students read and discuss theories.
- Organize students into small groups and have them read the theories about the disappearances of Amelia Earhart and Agatha Christie. Ask them to discuss which theory they think is the best, that is, the most convincing. Compare and discuss students' ideas as a whole class.

Answers
Answers will vary.

4 In your notebook, write another explanation for Earhart's and Christie's disappearances. Follow the steps below.
Students write alternative explanations for a mystery.
- Ask students to read again the stories about Amelia Earhart and Agatha Christie and the respective explanations. Have students work alone writing their own alternative accounts to explain the disappearances of Earhart and Christie. Remind students to use past modal verbs to express their ideas.
- Have students share and compare their theories in pairs and offer feedback.

Answers
Answers will vary.

Stop and Think! Critical Thinking
Work in small groups. Read your theories out loud. Which is the most credible? Why?
- Organize students into small groups and have them discuss which of their various theories they think is the most credible, that is, the most convincing or the most probable.
- Invite groups to share their comments with the rest of the class.

Wrap-up
Students create sentences using the Glossary items.
- Organize students into teams and challenge them, within a set time, to write sentences including each of the Glossary items in turn. Alternatively, have them write one single sentence using all of the items.

➡ **Workbook p. 145, Activity 3**

Preparing for the Next Lesson
Ask students to watch introductions to the Nazca Lines in Peru: http://goo.gl/ta1zqQ and http://goo.gl/yl8xmI.

Culture

Objective
Students will be able to discuss the Nazca Lines in Peru.

Lesson 7   Student's Book pp. 76 and 77

> ✔ **Homework Check!**
> Workbook p. 145, Activity 3
> **Answers**
> **3** Answer the following questions in your notebook. Then share your answers with the class.
> Answers will vary.

Warm-up
Students activate prior knowledge about Peru.
- With books closed, ask students to work in pairs and write down three facts about Peru. Compare and discuss their answers.

1 What do you know about the Nazca Lines? Discuss with a classmate. The captions of the pictures will help you.
Students activate knowledge about a topic.
- Ask students to look at the photos and the captions. Organize them into pairs and have them discuss what they have heard or read about the Nazca Lines. Invite students to share their ideas with the class.

2 Think Fast! Mention a strange or mysterious event or place in your country which scientists can't totally explain.
Students do a two-minute timed challenge: brainstorming examples of strange or mysterious events and places.
- Organize students into pairs or small groups and challenge them to think of instances of mysterious events or places in their own country. Compare and discuss their ideas.

3 Read an encyclopedia article about the Nazca Lines. Then complete the fact file.
Students summarize information from a text.
- Ask students to look at the text. Ask them how often they consult online encyclopedias such as Wikipedia, and for what purposes. Have students work alone reading the article and completing the Fact File below. Check answers.

Answers
top to bottom Nazca Desert (southern Peru), over 2,000 years ago, 500 km^2, animals and plants, 1920s, World Heritage Site

- Draw students' attention to the **Guess What!** box. Read aloud the information about World Heritage Sites and elicit observation and comment.

Extension
Students invent their own Nazca Lines designs.
- Ask students to create their own designs in the same style as the famous Nazca Lines. Invite individual students to present their drawings to the rest of the class, explaining what the figure is and what it represents.

Wrap-up
Students play a doodle game on the board.
- Organize students into two teams. A student from one team starts to draw a random shape or figure on the board, without saying what it is. Another member of the same team adds a little more to the drawing. At each step, players from the other team use modal verbs to speculate about what they think the drawing is. For example, *It might be an animal. It must be a horse.*

➡ **(No homework today.)**

Teaching Tip
Using Dictionaries
If possible, organize your class resources so that each student has (or has access to) a monolingual English dictionary. Make sure students know how to use it. If not, show them. Encourage students to refer to their dictionaries whenever appropriate during the lesson, though they should first try to figure out the meaning of a word from its context whenever possible.

Lesson 8 — Student's Book p. 77

Warm-up
Students review the spelling of key vocabulary items.
- Carry out a quick spelling test of words from the Wikipedia article about the Nazca Lines: *desert, mountains, commercial, archaeologists, weather, heritage, mystery,* etc.

4 🎧 [20] **Listen to two people talking about some possible explanations for the Nazca Lines. Complete the explanations with the words from the box.**

Students listen and complete sentences with key vocabulary items.
- Read aloud the first item and elicit the correct word to complete the sentence (roads). Then have students work alone or in pairs completing the rest of the activity. Check answers.

Answers
1. roads, 2. processions, 3. gods / sky,
4. map / planets, 5. Aliens

Audio Script
WOMAN: Listen, I saw this great documentary about the Nazca Lines last night… They are so interesting and mysterious.
MAN: Oh, you mean those drawings on the ground in a desert in Peru? They were roads built by the Incas, weren't they?
WOMAN: Well, that is one of the theories that explains the lines, but nobody really knows for sure why the drawings were made.
MAN: Oh, yeah?
WOMAN: Uh-huh. The most accepted theory suggests that the geoglyphs must have been paths for religious ceremonies. The Nazca people would march along them in procession.
MAN: That sounds interesting! What are the other theories?
WOMAN: Another theory holds that the Nazca might have made the drawings so that their gods could see their people from the sky, while another claims the lines could have been a type of astronomic map of planets and stars.
MAN: I see… What about the aliens?
WOMAN: Aliens??? What do you mean?
MAN: Aliens! Extraterrestrial creatures could have produced the geoglyphs, right? I've read about it somewhere, it is a theory some people believe in.
WOMAN: Come on, you must be kidding! Aliens couldn't have created the drawings simply because they don't exist!
MAN: Well, I don't know…

Stop and Think! Value
What is the best theory for the Nazca Lines? Why?
- Organize students into small groups and have them discuss which of the theories about the Nazca Lines they think is the best, that is, the most convincing. (If necessary, write ideas on the board to get them started.)
- Invite groups to share their ideas with the rest of the class.

Extension
Students write an imaginary account about the Nazca Lines.
- Ask students to imagine being one of the airline pilots who first saw the Nazca Lines from the air. Have them write the pilot's personal account of what he or she experienced that day.

Wrap-up
Students role-play conversations about the Nazca Lines.
- Organize students into pairs and have them role-play either a) a conversation between a visitor to Peru and a local resident who has some knowledge of the Nazca Lines or b) a conversation between two archaeologists about how and why the Nazca Lines were formed.

➡ **(No homework today.)**

Project

Objectives
Students will be able to make a presentation about an unsolved mystery.

Lesson 9
Student's Book pp. 78 and 79

Warm-up
Students brainstorm items related to crime and detectives.
- Organize students into pairs or small groups. Set a time limit and have them brainstorm the names of famous detectives, real-life detective agencies, detective TV shows, etc.

1 Look at the slides of a presentation about a famous unsolved mystery. Number the slides in the order you think they were presented.

Students number parts of a story in the correct order.
- Ask students to look at the sequence of slides. Elicit that they tell the story of a crime, in particular, a hijacking. Have students read through the information and number the slides in the order they think they were presented.

2 Now listen to the presentation. Check the order of the slides in Activity 1.

Students listen to check their answers to the previous activity.
- Ask students to listen to the presentation about an unsolved mystery and to check the sequence of the slides.

Answers
top to bottom, left to right 4, 6, 5, 1, 8, 7, 3, 9, 2

Audio Script
GIRL 1: Good morning, everyone. We're here today to talk about D. B. Cooper, an American man who is responsible for one of the most mysterious unsolved cases in the history of the FBI.

BOY 1: But who was D. B. Cooper? Well, nobody knows who he really was; his real identity was never discovered. In the afternoon of November 24 in 1971, he boarded a plane in Portland, Oregon. The plane was going to Seattle, Washington. The flight was scheduled to last 30 minutes.

GIRL 2: During the flight, Cooper gave a note to one of the flight attendants. According to FBI records, the note read: "I have a bomb in my briefcase. I will use it if necessary. I want you to sit next to me. You are being hijacked."

GIRL 1: The flight attendant sat next to Cooper, who made his demands. He wanted $200,000, four parachutes and a fuel truck to refuel the plane in Seattle. The flight attendant then informed the pilot about what was happening.

BOY 1: When the plane landed in Seattle, Cooper's demands were met. He released the passengers and most of the crew. Then it took off again, heading to Reno, a city in Nevada. Cooper asked the crew to remain in the cockpit. In the middle of the flight, a light turned on in the cockpit, indicating that one of the doors of the plane was opened.

GIRL 2: When the plane finally landed in Reno, Cooper was not found on it. He had jumped off the aircraft mid-air, somewhere between Seattle and Reno. Although extensive searches were done to locate Cooper, he was never found… nor the parachute, nor the money.

Extension
Students discuss theories about a crime mystery.
- Organize students into small groups and have them share and discuss their ideas about a) how they think D. B. Cooper escaped from the plane and b) what they think happened to him after he left the plane.

Wrap-up
Students act out a news bulletin about a crime mystery.
- Organize students into small groups and invite them to prepare a radio or TV news report about the case of D. B. Cooper or about some other crime.

Teaching Tip
Modeling Activities

Always model for students what they are expected to do or produce, especially when it comes to new skills or activities, by explaining and demonstrating the learning actions. Modeling promotes learning and motivation, as well as increasing student self-confidence. Students will have a stronger belief that they can accomplish a learning task if they follow steps that have been clearly demonstrated.

Lesson 10   Student's Book p. 79

Warm-up
Students play *How Many Words?*
- Write on the board a long word such as *archaeologist* or a phrase such as *unsolved mystery*. Challenge students to see how many words they can make using only letters from the word or phrase.

3 Work in small groups. Make a presentation about an unsolved mystery. Follow the steps below.
Students create presentations about unsolved mysteries.
- Ask students to read the three steps carefully, then organize them into small groups and have them start work on their presentations. Encourage students to present more than one theory to explain their chosen mystery. Encourage them to use past modal verbs (*must have, might have*, etc. + past participle) to speculate about possibilities. Remind students not to write out the whole text of their presentation on their slides, just the key words.

4 Ready? Make your presentation to the other groups.
Students present their work for the rest of the class.
- Invite students to share their presentations with the rest of the class.

Stop and Think! Critical Thinking
Which presentation did you like best? Why?
- Organize students into pairs and have them discuss which of the presentations they liked the best and why. Ask them to consider the content, the use of graphics and sound, the style, the delivery, the overall effect of the presentation, etc.
- Invite pairs to share their comments with the rest of the class.

The Digital Touch
To incorporate digital media in the project, suggest one or more of the following:
- Invite students to create their presentations using PowerPoint or similar slide show presentation programs.
- If possible, allow students to upload their work to the school's website.

Note that students should have the option to do a task on paper or digitally.

Wrap-up
Students speculate about the mysteries that they heard.
- Recap briefly the content of the presentations and invite students, as a whole-class activity, to speculate on what they think happened in each unsolved mystery case.

 Workbook p. 144, Activity 1 (Review)

# Review

Objective
Students will be able to consolidate their understanding of the vocabulary and grammar learned in the unit.

Lesson 11   Student's Book p. 80

> ✔ **Homework Check!**
> Workbook p. 144, Activity 1 (Review)
> **Answers**
> 1 Write a sentence speculating about what may have happened in each photo. Use a past modal and the appropriate vocabulary word.
> Answers will vary.

Warm-up
Students devise experiments to test extrasensory perception.
- Organize students into pairs or small groups and invite them to devise an experiment to test whether telekinesis, clairvoyance or telepathy really work. Have students share their ideas with the rest of the class.

1 Complete the sentences. Then number the pictures according to the description they refer to.
Students complete sentences and then match them with images.
- Read aloud the first item and elicit the correct answer (*Zombies*). Then have students work alone or in pairs completing the rest of the activity. Check answers.

Answers
1. Zombies, 2. aliens, 3. Werewolves, 4. ghosts;
left to right 4, 1, 2, 3

2 Complete the definitions with the correct word.
Students match words with definitions.
- Ask students to work in pairs matching each extrasensory perception word with the correct definition. Check answers by having students read the completed definitions aloud.

Answers
left to right Telekinesis, Clairvoyance, Telepathy

3 Decide if the sentences are right (R) or wrong (W), paying attention to the underlined words. Correct the wrong sentences.
Students read and check sentences for the correct use of vocabulary items.
- Ask students to read the sentences and to focus on the underlined words. Have them mark whether the words are right or wrong and have them correct the sentences that use the wrong word. Check answers.

Answers
1. R, 2. W, There are people who say they have been abducted by <u>aliens</u> and taken into their spaceships.
3. W, <u>Werewolves</u> are people who can transform into a wolf, usually when the moon is full.

Wrap-up
Students exchange accounts of extrasensory perception.
- Organize students into small groups and have them share accounts that they have heard or read about cases of telekinesis, clairvoyance or telepathy.

➤ **(No homework today.)**

> **Teaching Tip**
> **Getting Students' Attention**
> If you have a large group, you won't be easily heard if you try to talk over everyone, or else you will lose your voice! Simply have a certain place in the classroom where you go and stand when you want everyone's attention and go and stand in it. This could be in front of the board, facing the class or it could be near the door, or in the corner. Explain to students at the beginning of the course, "When I want your attention, I will stand here and you will stop what you are doing and listen to me. Is that clear?"

6 What would the world be like if…?

Grammar	Vocabulary
Third Conditional: <u>If</u> the astronauts <u>had stopped</u> their descent, they <u>might have crashed</u> into the Moon. **Mixed Conditional:** <u>If</u> scientists <u>hadn't mapped</u> the human genome, we <u>wouldn't understand</u> many genetic diseases	**Milestones of the 20th Century:** breakthrough, crisis, disaster, discovery, pandemic, revolution, war

Listening	Speaking
Listening to make predictions, listening for main ideas	Debating issues related to history and world events

What would the world be like if…?

In the first lesson, read the unit title aloud and have students look carefully at the unit cover. Encourage them to think about the message in the picture. At the end of the unit, students will discuss the big question: *What would the world be like if…?*

Teaching Tip
Monitoring Students in Speaking Activities
While the students are doing an activity, walk slowly around the classroom and listen to their conversations. Look at one pair while you are actually listening to a different pair nearby. Correct the pair nearby (who probably thought you were listening to the pair you were looking at) to keep everyone on their toes. If they do not know for sure when you are listening to them, they cannot switch off or revert to their mother tongue. Have a piece of paper and a pen with you as you move around the classroom so that you can jot down any recurring problems, which can then be dealt with at the end with the whole class.

Objective
Students will be able to use **milestones of the 20th century** vocabulary to talk about recent history.

Lesson 1
Student's Book pp. 84 and 85

Warm-up
Students speculate about photos of key events in 20th century history.
- Show students a series of photos showing a selection of landmark events in the 20th century, for example, scenes showing wars, revolutions, scientific achievements, discoveries, natural disasters, etc. Choose images that students may have some knowledge of. Invite them to comment and share what they know about the events in the photos.

1 Look at the timeline. Underline the correct option to complete the captions.
Students look at a timeline and select the correct words in the captions.
- Ask students to look at the timeline. Elicit or point out that a timeline is a graphical representation of a certain period of time and that it shows, in chronological order, important events that took place during that period. Referring to the title of the lesson, elicit or explain the origin and meaning of the term *milestone*.
- Ask students to read the caption for each photo and to underline the correct option. Check the answers.

Answers

in chronological order war, revolution, flu pandemic, discovery, breakthrough, crisis, war, discovery, crisis, disaster

2 Match the sentence halves.
Students match halves of sentences about 20th century milestones.
- Read aloud the first phrase and ask students to identify the phrase in the right-hand column that best completes it (*broke out in the first half of the 20th century, in 1914 and 1939.*), then have students work alone or in pairs completing the rest of the activity. Check answers by having students read the complete sentences aloud.

Answers

1. broke out in the first half of the 20th century, in 1914 and 1939. 2. the Russian Revolution in October, 1917. 3. the flu pandemic, which killed millions of people. 4. a major breakthrough with penicillin, in 1928. 5. its first global crisis, caused by the U.S. stock market crash. 6. was made by three British scientists, in 1953. 7. hit Ukraine, but it also affected other countries in Europe, in 1986.

- Draw students' attention to the **Guess What!** box. Read the information aloud and elicit observation and comment. Ask if students recognize the famous quote: "That's one small step for man and one giant leap for mankind."

3 Complete the chart with the underlined words from Activity 2.
Students complete a chart with key **milestones** vocabulary items.
- Ask students to look at the first item in the chart. Explain that *war breaks out* is a common collocation (words that are frequently found together). Have students complete the rest of the chart. Check the answers.

Answers

top to bottom war, led, pandemic, achieve, go through, discovery, disaster

Wrap-up
Students play a memory game with 20th century milestones.
- Organize students into two teams. One team mentions two milestone events and the other team has to say which happened first.

▶ **Workbook p. 146, Activities 1 and 2**

> **Teaching Tip**
> **Pairing Students for Fluency Activities**
> If you have some quiet students and some talkative ones, pair the quiet ones together for fluency activities (as opposed to vocabulary or grammar activities) to encourage them both to talk more. If you put a talkative student in a pair with a quiet one, there is the risk that the talkative one monopolizes the conversation while the quiet one happily allows this to happen.

Lesson 2 Student's Book p. 85

> ✔ Homework Check!
> Workbook p. 146, Activities 1 and 2
> Answers
> **1 Read and match.**
> 1. a, 2. e, 3. d, 4. b, 5. c
> **2 Read and circle the correct verb.**
> 1. led, 2. fight, 3. hit, 4. achieved

Warm-up
Students review the dates of certain 20th century milestones.
- With books closed, write on one side of the board a series of 20th century milestone events and on the other side, in random order, the years in which those events took place. Challenge students to match each event with the correct date.

4 🎧²² **Listen to two students talking about some of the events on the timeline. Number the ones they mention.**
Students listen for key ideas.
- Ask students to look at the list of timeline events. Then ask students to listen to the audio and number the items in the list that are mentioned. Check answers.

Answers
1. Discovery of penicillin, 2. Second World War, 3. Invention of computers, 4. Invention of the Internet

Audio Script
HARRY: The history class about the milestones of the 20th century was so interesting!
ASHLEY: It sure was! And I agree with Mr. Raymond about the most important events.
HARRY: Do you?
ASHLEY: Yeah! The most important milestone was the discovery of penicillin, definitely! Antibiotics have saved millions of lives.
HARRY: Hmm... I'm not so sure... In my opinion, the Second World War was much more important. Millions of people died and the atomic bombs on Hiroshima and Nagasaki were an awful event...
ASHLEY: I agree... but antibiotics prevented the deaths of other millions of soldiers on the battlefield.
HARRY: Well, you're right about *that*.
ASHLEY: How about the invention of computers? Was that important?
HARRY: Of course it was! Computers have changed the world!
ASHLEY: I don't know... I think the Internet was much more significant.
HARRY: Ashley, the Internet only exists because computers were invented...
ASHLEY: Oops... you're so right! Maybe I need to attend Mr. Raymond's class again.

5 Answer the questions below.
Students discuss questions related to 20th century events.
- Ask students to work alone answering the questions with their own ideas.

Answers
Answers will vary.

6 Share your ideas in Activity 5 with another classmate.
Students compare and discuss their ideas in pairs.
- Organize students into pairs and have them share and discuss their ideas from Activity 5. Then open up the discussion with the whole class.

Stop and Think! Critical Thinking
In your opinion, what was the most important event of the 20th century? Why?
- Organize students into small groups and have them discuss what they think was the most important event of the 20th century. Encourage them to give their reasons.
- Invite groups to share their comments with the rest of the class.

> ### Extension
> Students research 20th century milestones in their own country.
> - Organize students into pairs or small groups and invite them to look for information about key 20th century events in their own country.
> - Have students share their presentations with the rest of the class.

Wrap-up
Students review collocations on this page.
- Read out a verb from the chart in Activity 3 and ask students to supply a noun or noun phrase that goes with it.

➡ **Workbook pp. 146 and 147, Activities 3 and 4**

Grammar

Objectives
Students will be able to use **third conditional** and **mixed conditional** to talk about alternate realities.

Lesson 3   Student's Book pp. 86 and 87

> ✔ **Homework Check!**
> Workbook pp. 146 and 147, Activities 3 and 4
> **Answers**
> **3 Match the sentence halves.**
> 1. e, 2. a, 3. d, 4. b
> **4 Complete the quotes using a word below.**
> *left to right, top to bottom* economic, discovery, war, revolution

Warm-up
Students identify statements as true or false.
- Read aloud a series of statements from the 20th century timeline on the previous pages, some true and some false. Ask students to raise their hands when they hear a false statement. Then have them try to correct the statement.

1 Read the article. Then read the hypothetical statements and mark (✓) what really happened.
Students consider other possible outcomes regarding the Apollo 11 mission and infer what really happened.
- Ask students to read the five hypothetical sentences. Tell them that, in different words, they are part of the text they have already read.
- Have students mark what really happened, that is, the sentences that reflect reality.
- Tell them that they must read both possibilities carefully and that although they can sound similar, they must be cautious because they mean quite different things.
- You can start reading the first sentence in a different order—the result sentence first and then the part with the hypotetical past condition, this might help students to identify the hypothetical part of the sentence.

Answers
1. a, 2. a, 3. b, 4. a, 5. a

2 Read and match.
Students identify conditions and characteristics in conditional sentences.
- Ask students to match the sentences according to what the yellow box indicates regarding the third conditional.

Answers
1. We use the third conditional to talk about things that could have happened, but didn't. 2. We use *had* and the past participle in the condition part of the sentence. 3. We use *would* and the present perfect in the result part of the sentence. 4. We can also use *could* and *might* in place of *would* in the sentence.

- Draw students' attention to the **Guess What!** box. Read the information aloud and elicit observation and comment. Ask students if they understand what a *mixed conditional* is and when they can use it. Give examples.

- Draw students' attention to the box with information about the **Third Conditional** and clarify any doubts that students may have about form or meaning. Check that students understand the concept of an unreal, that is, a hypothetical situation.

Wrap-up
Students speculate about alternate personal histories.
- Have students talk in pairs discussing alternate events in their life, for example, *If I had been born in London…*

 Workbook p. 147, Activities 1 and 2

> **Teaching Tip**
> **Reading Instructions Aloud**
> If students read instructions silently, they all finish at different times. But if they listen to one student reading them aloud, they all finish at the same time.

Lesson 4 Student's Book p. 87

✔ **Homework Check!**
Workbook p. 147, Activities 1 and 2
Answers
1 Read and mark (✓) the correct verb.
1. might have been, 2. would not be, 3. would not have been killed, 4. would not have been destroyed
2 Complete the sentences using the correct form of the verb in parentheses.
1. would have had, 2. had not practiced, 3. wouldn't be, 4. had not joined, 5. would not have been

Warm-up
Students review past participle forms.
- As a whole class, conduct a quick-fire oral quiz to test students' recall of the past participle forms of irregular verbs (*won, fallen*, etc.).

3 Write the correct forms of the verbs to complete the sentences.
Students complete conditional sentences.
- Read aloud the first item and elicit the correct forms of the given verbs sentence (*hadn't used*), then have students work alone or in pairs completing the rest of the activity. Check the answers.

Answers
1. hadn't used, 2. wouldn't have been able, 3. hadn't mapped, 4. hadn't discovered

Stop and Think! Critical Thinking
Think of some facts about the past and make some hypotheses. What could have happened if things had been different?
- Organize students into small groups and have them discuss possible answers to questions 1 to 5 in Activity 1. Encourage them to be imaginative.
- Invite groups to share their ideas with the rest of the class.

> **Extension**
> Students research about Christopher Columbus and his trips to America.
> - Ask students to look for information about Columbus and his trips to this continent.
> - Have students present their results with sentences using the third conditional, for instance, *If Columbus hadn't come to America, Europeans wouldn't have become colonists.*

Wrap-up
Students compile lists of irregular verbs.
- Ask students to write as many irregular verbs as they can recall.
- Ask them to write them down in their present base form, next to it its simple past form and then the past participle.
- Encourage them to list them alphabetically.
- Have them present to the class the verbs they were able to write down; check that they are written correctly and see how many verbs are repeated.

 Workbook p. 148, Activities 3 and 4

> **Teaching Tip**
> **Organizing Students for Pairwork**
> With an odd number of students, don't pair the extra student up with yourself—make a group of three. This way, you will be able to give your attention to the whole group and monitor their work properly.

Listening & Speaking

Objectives
Students will be able to **listen to make predictions, listen for main ideas** and debate issues related to world events.

Lesson 5   Student's Book p. 88

✔ **Homework Check!**
Workbook p. 148, Activities 3 and 4

Answers
3 Complete the sentences with your own ideas.
Answers will vary.
4 Make sentences about what the world would be like if the following things hadn't been invented. Share your ideas with a partner.
Answers will vary.

Warm-up
Students review acronyms for countries and organizations.
- As a quick-fire quiz, test students' knowledge of acronyms like NATO, USA, UN, etc.

1 Look at the pictures. Then read the statements and circle *Yes* or *No*.
Students make predictions about a text.
- Ask students to look at the pictures and to think about the situation. Have them mark the two statements *Yes* or *No*. Check the answers.

Answers
1. No, 2. No

2 🎧²³ Listen to the beginning of one of Professor Gardner's classes. Is he going to talk about a real war? Discuss with a partner.
Students listen and predict content.
- Ask students to listen to the audio and discuss whether the professor is talking about a war that actually happened or not. Discuss answers.

Audio Script
PROFESSOR GARDNER: Cold… war… This is a war that never happened. But if it had actually happened, I believe we probably wouldn't be here now, because nuclear weapons, which could have been used by the United States and the Soviet Union, would have destroyed the world.

3 🎧²⁴ One of the students in Professor Gardner's class is taking notes. Listen to another excerpt of the class and number the notes in the order the ideas are mentioned.
Students listen for main ideas.
- Ask students to listen to the professor and to number the notes in the order they are mentioned. Check the answers.

Answers
top to bottom, left to right 4, 6, 1, 5, 3, 7, 2

Audio Script
PROFESSOR GARDNER: As you probably know, the United States and the Soviet Union were allies during the Second World War, but their friendship turned into deep rivalry and distrust right after its end. Americans were totally against communism. Soviets claimed Americans took too long to enter the war in Europe, an attitude that, in their opinion, caused the deaths of millions of Russians. After the war, the Russians occupied many countries in Eastern Europe, such as Poland, Hungary and Romania. This attitude made Americans even angrier at the Russians. They thought they were planning to control the world. On the Soviet side, Russians didn't like American interference in other countries and the accumulation of nuclear weapons. The hostile relationship led to an unprecedented arms race and the beginning of the Atomic Age. The most difficult moment in the relations between the Soviet Union and the United States was a 13-day period in October, 1962, known as the Cuban Missile Crisis, when the world got very close to a new global war.
MALE STUDENT: Professor Gardner, can I ask a question?
PROFESSOR GARDNER: Sure!
MALE STUDENT: What would have happened if the Russians insisted on installing nuclear weapons in Cuba?
PROFESSOR GARDNER: I think that the United States would have attacked Cuba and the Third World War would have started. According to historians…

Wrap-up
Students give oral summaries of events.
- Ask students to give an oral summary of the events explained in the audio.

➤ **Workbook p. 149, Activities 1 and 2**

Lesson 6   Student's Book p. 89

> ✔ **Homework Check!**
> Workbook p. 149, Activities 1 and 2
> **Answers**
> **1 What do you know about the Fukushima nuclear disaster? Discuss the answers to the following questions with a partner. Then read and check your answers.**
> 1. March 11, 2011, off the northeastern coast of Japan. 2. The nuclear power plant was flooded by a tsunami, causing a nuclear meltdown and the release of radioactive material. 3. It was the second largest nuclear disaster after Chernobyl.
> **2 Mark each statement *T* (True) or *F* (False).**
> 1. T, 2. F (It was the second largest nuclear disaster after Chernobyl.), 3. F (Many of these people are still displaced.), 4. T, 5. T

Warm-up
Students review the spelling of key vocabulary items.
- Carry out a quick spelling test of key words from information on page 88: *communism, hostile, missile, nuclear, interference,* etc.

4 🎧24 **Listen to the class once more. Write F if the statement represents a fact and O if it represents an opinion.**
Students distinguish between facts and opinions.
- Ask students to read all of the statements, then have them listen to the audio again and mark each statement as a fact or an opinion. When checking answers, encourage students to say what they heard in the audio that helped them to decide that a statement was an opinion.

Answers
1. O, 2. F, 3. O, 4. O, 5. O

- Draw students' attention to the **Guess What!** box on page 88. Read the information aloud and elicit observation and comment.

5 You are going to discuss an issue in groups. Follow the steps below.
Students take part in a planned group discussion.
- Ask students to read all the instructions, then organize students into groups of six and ask them to follow the three steps. For Step 3, elicit or provide students with other expressions that they can use to make a point, to correct themselves, to interrupt someone, or to ask for clarification.

Draw students' attention to the **Be Strategic!** box and ask them to read the information. Point out the phrases that show when someone is expressing an opinion.

Stop and Think! Critical Thinking
Was it easy to discuss the issue with your classmates? What could you do to improve teamwork the next time you do an activity like the one above?
- Organize students into small groups and have them discuss how easy it was to discuss their chosen topic and what they could do to improve the way they work in the future.
- Invite groups to share their comments with the rest of the class.

> ### Extension
> Students devise a history syllabus for their school.
> - Organize students into small groups and invite them to devise a history syllabus for each year of high school, including 20th century milestones.

Wrap-up
Students role-play conversations between former enemies.
- Organize students into pairs and have them role-play conversations between citizens of nations that were once enemies or rivals, exploring the issues that divided the two countries.

➡ **Workbook p. 149, Activity 3**

Preparing for the Next Lesson
Ask students to watch a short introduction to Portugal's Age of Exploration: goo.gl/57I6u4 or invite them to consult the following website: goo.gl/Jid9hF

Culture

Objective
Students will be able to understand and discuss Portugal's Age of Exploration.

Lesson 7   Student's Book pp. 90 and 91

> ✔ **Homework Check!**
> Workbook p. 149, Activity 3
> **Answers**
> 3 Research about another famous nuclear disaster. In your notebook, write about:
> Answers will vary.

Warm-up
Students compare maps and brainstorm differences.
- With books closed, show students an old map of the world and elicit ways in which maps have changed and improved over time.
- Then ask students to look at the map on page 90 and elicit observation and comment.

1 What do you know about the people in the pictures and the situations depicted in them? Discuss with a classmate.
Students activate prior knowledge of a topic.
- Ask students to look at the images and their accompanying captions and the map on page 90. Organize students into pairs and ask them to discuss the information. Ask them to consider in which historical period they think the figures in the statues lived. Elicit observation and comment about their dress, their pose, the objects that they are holding, etc.

2 Read an extract from an e-book about the Portuguese discoveries. Check if any of your ideas from Activity 1 are mentioned.
Students read a text and compare its content with their existing ideas.
- Ask students to read the extract. Organize students into pairs and have them comment on which of the key points mentioned in the text coincide with the ideas that they came up with in the previous activity.
- As a whole-class activity compare and discuss students' ideas. Clarify any key concepts for students who may be less familiar with this period in history.

Extension
Students research countries where Portuguese is spoken.
- Organize students into small groups and invite them to prepare a presentation, including maps, about countries in the world where Portuguese is the sole official language (Portugal, Angola, Brazil, Cape Verde, Guinea-Bissau, Mozambique, Sao Tomé and Príncipe). Ask them to show how Portuguese in Portugal is different from Portuguese in, for example, Brazil.

Wrap-up
Students play *How Many Words?*
- Write on the board a long word such as *discoveries* or a phrase such as *age of exploration*. Challenge students to see how many words they can make using just letters from the word or phrase.

▶ **(No homework today.)**

 Teaching Tip
Improving Pronunciation
Helping students to improve their pronunciation is very important. There is little point in their learning a new word, what it means and how to use it in a sentence, if other people find it hard to understand them due to their pronunciation.

Lesson 8 — Student's Book p. 91

Warm-up

Students recap facts about Portugal's Age of Exploration.
- With books closed and as a whole class, quiz students on some of the facts found on pages 90 and 91. For example, ask, *Where is the Monument to the Discoveries?* (Lisbon) or, *When did Portuguese expansion begin?* (1419)

3 🎧²⁵ **Listen to a recording of the book chapter in Activity 2. Complete the timeline with the words in the box.**
Students listen for specific information to complete a text.
- Ask students to read the book chapter again and to think about the type of word they think goes in each space: the name of a person, a place, etc.
- Then have students listen to the audio and complete the text with the correct items from the box. Check answers by asking students to read aloud the completed sentences from the text.

Answers

South Africa, route, Portugal, Africa, India, port, trade, Australia, John III, Chinese

---

Audio Script

Chapter 15 – The Portuguese and Their Discoveries

In the 15th and 16th centuries, the Portuguese set out to explore and conquer new territories, which led them to make significant discoveries in the Americas, Africa and Asia. They also traced important maritime routes and mapped the coasts of several countries. The Portuguese were so powerful and skilled that in less than a century their empire had extended to four different continents.

The Portuguese expansion started in 1419, with several expeditions mapping the coast of West Africa. After that, the Portuguese set several exploration milestones:

1489
Bartolomeu Dias reached the Cape of Good Hope (in today's South Africa) and entered the Indian Ocean.
1498
Vasco da Gama sailed along the coast of Africa to reach India, setting out a trade route between India and Portugal.
1500
Pedro Alvares Cabral landed in Brazil and claimed the territory for Portugal.
1506
Tristao da Cunha made landfall on Madagascar, an island off of the east coast of Africa.
1510
Alfonso de Albuquerque conquered Goa, an important city in India.
1511
Alfonso de Albuquerque conquered Malacca, a major trade port in Malaysia.
1513
Jorge Alvares reached China and established trade with the Chinese.
1521
Cristovao de Mendonca discovered Australia.
1530
John III, King of Portugal, began the colonization of Brazil.
1557
The Portuguese settled permanently in Macau, a Chinese territory.

Stop and Think! Value

Do you know any famous explorers from other countries? If you do, what can you say about them?
- Organize students into small groups and have them discuss any famous explorers that they know about from other countries (Leif Ericson, Marco Polo, John Cabot, Jacque Cartier, Francis Drake, Henry Hudson, James Cook, etc.).
- Invite groups to share their ideas with the rest of the class.

Wrap-up

Students play a quiz game about dates.
- Organize students into two teams. A player from one team mentions a key name of place or event from the book chapter on page 91 and players from the other team have to give the correct year. For example, *Alfonso de Albuquerque conquered Goa.* (1510)

▶ **(No homework today.)**

 **Project**

Objective
Students will be able to create an online newspaper home page.

Lesson 9   Student's Book pp. 92 and 93

Warm-up
Students brainstorm the main sections of an online newspaper.
- Show the class two or three examples of online national newspapers with today's news. Elicit the main sections of a typical newspaper website —news, sports, reviews, weather, cartoons, etc. Ask students if they ever consult online newspapers and if so, which ones.

1 **Look at the front page of an online newspaper. Match the sections to the descriptions below.**
Students match parts of an online newspaper with short descriptions.
- Ask students to look at the front page of the online newspaper on page 92. Read aloud the first description and ask students to say the number of the section that it refers to (7), then have students work in pairs completing the rest of the activity. Check the answers.

Answers

top to bottom 7, 3, 1, 4, 6, 2, 5

2 **Answer the questions about the front page.**
Students answer general comprehension questions.
- Ask students to work in pairs answering questions about the front page of the online newspaper. Check and discuss their answers. Some suggestions: *It is not a real front page because it is dated in the future. The headlines are all in the present simple and they all deal with good news. Readers can look for news stories using the search box at the top right of the page.*

Answers

Answers will vary.

Extension
Students research online newspapers in their country.
- Organize students into small groups and invite them to research and present information about the most important and most popular national newspapers in their own country. Encourage them to show examples of the front pages of different online newspapers.

Wrap-up
Students write national headlines for the year 2047.
- Organize students into pairs and invite them to write headlines for news stories about their own country for the year 2047. Have them include a variety of topics—politics, scientific breakthroughs, sports, entertainment, etc.

 Teaching Tip

Dealing With Large Numbers of Students
In large classes, students sometimes feel too shy to ask questions in class. It is important to allocate a certain time when they can come and see you for any extra help or to ask questions. Alternatively, try creating an online group using a chat application. Students can also use this online group to practice their English.

Lesson 10 Student's Book p. 93

Warm-up

Students complete real headlines with the missing words.
- Bring to class a selection of real headlines from today's (or recent) newspapers, but with one word deleted. Challenge students to supply the missing word using their knowledge of current events of by using context clues within the rest of the headline.

3 Work in small groups. You and your classmates are going to prepare the home page of an online newspaper for a future date. Follow the steps below.
Students create their own front page for an online newspaper.
- Ask students to read through all the steps carefully, then organize them into small groups and have them allocate different tasks to different members of the group before they start working.
- Tell students to give a lot of thought to the points in Step 4 of the instructions. Remind students to use the present simple for their headlines. Also, encourage them to use the third conditional to discuss what would have happened if a particular event had not taken place.

4 Share your newspaper home page with other groups.
Students present and share their online newspapers with their classmates.
- Invite students to share their online newspapers with the rest of the class.

Stop and Think! Critical Thinking

Which newspaper home page was the most interesting? Why?
- Organize students into pairs and have them discuss which of the online newspaper front pages they found the most interesting and why. Also, ask them to say which newspaper had the most varied content, the best graphic design and layout, the best name and logo, the best photos and images, etc.
- Invite pairs to share their comments with the rest of the class.

The Digital Touch

To incorporate digital media in the project, suggest one or more of the following:
- Invite students to create their online newspapers using free website builder services or by using PowerPoint or similar slide show presentation programs.
- If possible, allow students to upload their work to the school's website.

Note that students should have the option to do a task on paper or digitally.

Wrap-up

Students role-play news interviews.
- Organize students into pairs or groups of three and have them role-play conversations in which a newspaper reporter gathers information about a news story by interviewing eyewitnesses. Students can use stories that they include in their online newspapers or invent new ones.
- Have students share their role plays with the rest of the group.

▶ **Workbook p. 148, Activity 1 (Review)**

Review

Objective
Students will be able to consolidate their understanding of the vocabulary and grammar learned in the unit.

Lesson 11   Student's Book p. 94

> ✔ **Homework Check!**
> Workbook p. 148, Activity 1 (Review)
>
> **Answers**
> **1 Are the sentences correct (C) or incorrect (I)? Correct the incorrect sentences.**
> 1. I, ~~would be saved~~, would have been saved, 2. C, 3. I, ~~had led~~, hadn't led, 4. C

Warm-up
Students review the spelling of key vocabulary items.
- Carry out a quick spelling test of words for describing important historical events: *revolution, pandemic, discovery, breakthrough, crisis, disaster…*

1 Mark (✓) the correct alternative to complete the sentences. Pay attention to the words in bold.
Students select the correct collocations to complete sentences.
- Read aloud the first item and elicit the correct answer (*achieved*), then have students work alone or in pairs completing the rest of the activity by selecting the correct word or phrase for each space. Check answers by having students read the completed sentences aloud.

Answers
1. achieved, 2. having gone through, 3. will break out, 4. made, 5. led, 6. fight, 7. has ever hit

2 Complete the sentences with a collocation from the box. Pay attention to the verb form.
Students complete sentences with the correct collocations.
- Ask students to look at the first item. Elicit the correct answer (*made, discovery*). Point out that the verb has to be in the past simple tense, then have students work alone or in pairs completing the rest of the activity. Check answers by having students read the completed sentences aloud.

Answers
1. made / discovery, 2. achieved / breakthrough, 3. disaster / hit, 4. fight / pandemic

3 Match the sentences in Activity 2 to the pictures below.
Students match sentences with images.
- Ask students to look at the photos. Ask them to say which sentence from Activity 2 the first photo depicts (4), then have students work alone or in pairs completing the rest of the activity. Check the answers.

Answers
left to right 4, 3, 1, 2

Wrap-up
Students write their own sentences using collocations related to historical milestones.
- Write the following phrases on the board: *lead a revolution, fight a war, go through a crisis, make a discovery, fight a pandemic, achieve a breakthrough.* Challenge students to write a series of true sentences about milestone historical events using each collocation at least once.

 (No homework today.)

> **Teaching Tip**
> **Highlighting Stress in a Word**
> To practice stress placement, write the word in question on the board and ask students how many syllables it has. Ask them which is the stressed (strong) syllable. Write the stressed syllable in capital letters. For example:
> *pandemic* = 3 syllables, panDEMic.
> The second syllable is stressed.
> *breakthrough* = 2 syllables, BREAKthrough.
> The first syllable is stressed.

Lesson 12   Student's Book p. 95

Warm-up
Students choose a period in history to travel back in time to.
- Ask students to choose a period in history that they would like to visit if they had the power to travel back in time. Discuss various suggestions and encourage students to speculate about hypothetical situations using conditional sentences.

4 Are the sentences correct (C) or incorrect (I)? Correct the incorrect sentences.

Students make grammatical corrections to third conditional and mixed conditional sentences.
- Read aloud the first sentence and ask students to say if it is grammatically correct (C) or incorrect (I), then have students work alone or in pairs marking the sentences as correct or incorrect. Have students correct the incorrect sentences with the correct conditional forms. Check the answers.

Answers
1. C, 2. I, ~~haven't~~, hadn't, 3. I, ~~win~~, won, 4. C, 5. C, 6. I, ~~would have been~~, would be

5 Use the prompts and the images to write conditional sentences.

Students write conditional sentences from visual prompts.
- Ask students to look at the series of images. Elicit or explain that they show key personal milestones in the life of a person (shown in the last photo) and her grandfather and her great-grandparents. Make clear that students are going to use conditionals to talk hypothetically about things that did not actually happen.
- Have students look at the first image and read the sentence. Make clear the meaning by saying, *Mark was 18 and he fought in the Second World War, but if he hadn't been 18, he wouldn't have fought.* Have students work alone or in pairs writing conditional sentences for the remaining images. Check and discuss the answers.

Answers
1. If he hadn't fought in WW II, he wouldn't have gone to France. 2. If he hadn't gone to France, he wouldn't have met Marie. 3. If Mark and Marie hadn't met, they wouldn't have gotten married. 4. If they hadn't met and gotten married, they wouldn't have had my grandpa, James. 5. If my grandpa hadn't been born, I wouldn't be here in France today!

Extension
Students vote for key events and figures from their country's recent past.
- Organize students into groups and have them draw up nominations for their country for Person of the 20th Century and Key Event of the 20th Century.
- Compile a ballot form and have the class vote for the people and events that they think were the most important and influential in their country's recent history.

Big Question

Students are given the opportunity to revisit the Big Question and reflect on it.
- Ask students to turn to the unit opener on page 83 and to look at the pictures. Elicit observation and comment about what the images represent (*clockwise, from top left*: scientific/medical breakthroughs, world wars, space exploration, World Wide Web, development of computers).
- Read the question aloud. Discuss how questions like this enable us to speculate about how things could have been if history had taken a different course.
- As a whole class, discuss how hypothetical questions about the past can help us to better understand and to learn valuable lessons from history.

Scorecard
Hand out (and/or project) a *Scorecard*. Have students fill in their *Scorecards* for this unit.

➡ **Study for the unit test.**

7 What do I need to live abroad?

Grammar
Direct Speech: "She's going away for the summer." **Reported Speech:** Jake said (that) Katie was going away for the summer.

Vocabulary
Living and Studying Abroad: language school, local food, passport, plane tickets, student visa, travel arrangements, travel insurance

Reading
Identifying text types, reading for specific information

Writing
Writing an information leaflet

What do I need to live abroad?

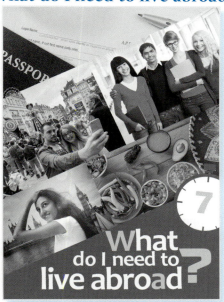

In the first lesson, read the unit title aloud and have students look carefully at the unit cover. Encourage them to think about the message in the picture. At the end of the unit, students will discuss the big question: *What do I need to live abroad?*

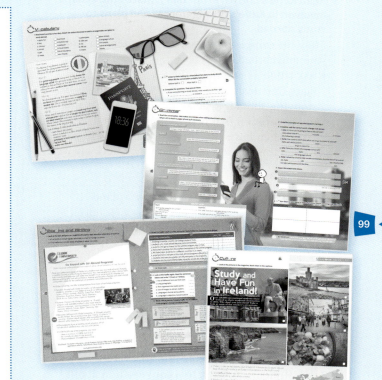

Teaching Tip
Teaching Teenagers
Use current, up-to-date and, where possible, authentic material to increase motivation and personalization. Let students bring some of their world into the classroom. Show an interest in teen culture but do not try to play teenager, as if you were one of them! The teacher represents authority and this distinction needs to be kept clear at all times. Exploit natural, spontaneous communication as it emerges in class and respond to this. Regarding resources, look for ready-made, teen-friendly lessons on YouTube since this is a medium that teenagers can respond to easily. Song lyrics sites are good for students to try out at home.

 Vocabulary

Objective
Students will be able to use **living abroad** to talk about living and studying abroad.

Lesson 1
Student's Book pp. 98 and 99

Warm-up
Students brainstorm a series of actions.
- Have students work in small groups brainstorming a list of things that they would need to do before starting a course of study abroad.

1 Read Katie's entries in her diary. Match the actions involved in Katie's arrangements and plans to study abroad.
Students complete phrases related to living and studying abroad.
- Ask students to look at the text. Elicit that it is a diary that deals with a person's preparations for studying abroad. Read aloud the first item and elicit the collocation that best combines with it (a student visa). Then have students work alone or in pairs completing the rest of the activity. Check answers.

Answers

1. apply for / a student visa, 2. buy / plane tickets, 3. choose / a language school, 4. enroll / in a course, 5. get / a passport, 6. make / travel arrangements, 7. participate / in local events, 8. take out / travel insurance, 9. try / local food, 10. fill out / forms, 11. make / new friends

2 ²⁶ Listen to Katie talking to a friend about her plans to study abroad. When did the conversation probably take place?
Students listen for specific information.
- Ask students to listen to a conversation about planning to study abroad. Have them look at Katie's diary and then determine which day she is talking about. Check answer.

Answer

Before April 12

Audio Script
JAKE: So... Tell me, Katie... Is it true you're going to France this summer?
KATIE: It is! I'm so excited about it!
JAKE: I can imagine! Is everything ready for your trip?
KATIE: Not really... I've done a lot, but I still have some things to do.
JAKE: I see... Have you bought the plane tickets?
KATIE: Not yet. I'll do that on the weekend with my mom. I need her credit card to do that, you know.
JAKE: Hehehe... I have my own credit card, and I'll get a car this summer...
KATIE: Yeah, but your parents don't even allow you to go to school by yourself, let alone travel to another country...

JAKE: OK, OK... And have you chosen the school yet?
KATIE: Yes, I'm going to study at French Plus. The reviews about it on the Internet were great.
JAKE: And are you going to Paris?
KATIE: Of course I am! I asked the school about weekend trips, but they haven't answered yet.
JAKE: I bet they have something planned for the students. Paris is a very romantic city, you know...
KATIE: Definitely! But I haven't gotten a student visa yet...
JAKE: How come?
KATIE: I spent the weekend gathering documents to apply for it. I couldn't find my school bulletin. But I'll take all the documents and forms to the French consulate today. Hey, why don't you come with me after school? We can discuss this history project on the way...
JAKE: Great idea! I'd love to spend more time with you, Katie...

Wrap-up
Students talk about studying abroad.
- Ask students to look at the "List of things I'd like to do while in Provence" at the foot of Katie's diary. Then organize them into pairs and have them exchange ideas about what they personally would like to do if they were visiting Provence or some other place.

▶ **Workbook p. 150, Activities 1 and 2**

 Teaching Tip

Using Synonyms to Elicit Vocabulary
Try using synonyms to elicit vocabulary. Make a statement and ask students to paraphrase it by using a synonym (or an antonym). Alternatively, pretend you have forgotten the word you are trying to elicit, something that happens regularly in natural conversation. Ask students questions to try to elicit the vocabulary that you are trying to remember.

Lesson 2 Student's Book p. 99

> ✔ **Homework Check!**
> Workbook p. 150, Activities 1 and 2
> **Answers**
> **1 Choose the verb to complete the sentences.**
> 1. apply for, 2. get, 3. choose, 4. enroll in,
> 5. fill out, 6. buy, 7. make, 8. try, 9. participate
> **2 Complete the dialogue with the correct part of the collocation.**
> 1. apply for, 2. take out, 3. buy, 4. choose,
> 5. enroll, 6. make, 7. try, 8. participate

Warm-up
Students practice collocations related to living and studying abroad.
- Write on the board a number of verbs from Activity 1 and ask students to supply a phrase that forms an appropriate collocation. For example, say *enroll* to elicit *in a course*.

3 Complete the questions. Then answer them.
Students complete questions about studying abroad and then answer them.
- Ask students to look at the questions. Elicit that the first two questions are in the second conditional, which students studied in Unit 4. Have students complete the questions using vocabulary items from the previous page. Then ask them to answer the questions using their own ideas.

Answers
1. passport (student visa), language school,
2. course, 3. travel insurance, 4. local events
Answers will vary.

- Draw students' attention to the **Guess What!** box. Read the information aloud and elicit observation and comment. Ask students if they have ever met a student from China.

4 Work in small groups. Share your answers in Activity 3 with your classmates.
Students share and compare their answers to Activity 3.
- Organize students into small groups and have them share and compare their answers to the questions in Activity 3. Then open up the discussion for the whole class.

Stop and Think! Critical Thinking
Is there anything else Katie should do before traveling to France?
- Organize students into small groups and have them discuss other things that they think Katie should do before she travels to France.
- Invite groups to share their ideas with the rest of the class.

> **Extension**
> Students present information about foreign students in their country.
> - Organize students into small groups and ask them to look for information about students in their country who come from abroad: numbers of foreign students in universities, exchange programs, places where people come to study the students' first language but as a foreign language, etc.

Wrap-up
Students role-play conversations about plans to study abroad.
- Organize students into pairs and have them role-play conversations in which one person is skeptical about the idea of studying abroad and their friend tries to persuade them that it is a good thing to do.

▶ **Workbook p. 150, Activity 3**

 Grammar

Objective
Students will be able to use **reported speech** to report indirectly what people said.

Lesson 3 Student's Book pp. 100 and 101

✔ **Homework Check!**
Workbook p. 150, Activity 3

Answers
3 Choose the correct order of events to study abroad.
1. a, 2. a, 3. b, 4. b

Warm-up
Students carry out an on-the-spot survey about text messaging.
- Ask students to look at the page. Elicit that it shows a text conversation. Ask students to think of questions that they can ask of each other to find out how, when, how much, how often, why, in what circumstances, etc. students text people.

1 Read the conversation. Jake makes one mistake when talking about Katie's plans. What is it? Go back to pages 98 and 99 if necessary.
Students read a text and find a factual error.
- Ask students to skim briefly through the text. Elicit or point out that it is a text conversation between two friends who are talking about Katie's plans to go to France to study French. Ask students to read the text and identify one factual error that Jake makes. Allow students to refer to Katie's diary on the previous pages if necessary. Check the answer.

Answer
Katie will study in Aix-en-Provence, not in Paris.

- Draw students' attention to the box with information about **Direct Speech** and **Reported Speech** and clarify any doubts that students may have about form or meaning.

2 Underline examples of reported speech in Activity 1.
Students identify instances of reported speech in a text.
- Ask students to look at the conversation on the opposite page. Have them underline examples of reported speech. Check answers and elicit the two verbs that are used in these instances for reporting someone's comments (*say, tell*).

Answers
She said she will study French in Paris., I told her I'm going to get a new car…, Katie said she hasn't got a visa yet…, she said she wants to discuss the history project on the way.

3 Complete with the correct words. Change verb tenses.
Students complete sentences with the correct verb forms.
- Ask students to quickly skim through the whole series of direct speech items. Then read aloud the first item and elicit the correct verb forms to change the direct speech into reported speech (*was, was going*). Then ask students to work alone or in pairs completing the rest of the activity. Check answers.

Answers
1. was / was going, 2. didn't / allow him / himself, 3. asked / if / had / chosen, 4. said / had asked / hadn't answered

Wrap-up
Students convert direct speech to reported speech and vice versa.
- Organize students into teams and ask them to write a series of sentences in direct speech and in reported speech. Have teams convert each other's sentences from direct speech to reported speech (or vice versa) in a set time limit.

➡ Workbook p. 151, Activities 1 and 2

 Teaching Tip
Modeling and Practicing Pronunciation Items
First, model the word or phrase yourself, in a normal way and at normal speed. Then ask students to repeat it after you, all together in chorus, until they can pronounce it acceptably. Then model the word or phrase again and ask individual students to repeat it after you.

Lesson 4 Student's Book p. 101

> ✔ **Homework Check!**
> Workbook p. 151, Activities 1 and 2
>
> **Answers**
> **1 Match the direct speech to the verb tense changes in reported speech.**
> 1. a, 2. d, 3. c
> **2 Mark (✓) the correct sentence in direct speech.**
> 1. 2, 2. 1, 3. 2, 4. 1, 5. 1

Warm-up
Students identify direct speech and reported speech.
- Read aloud a series of examples of direct speech and reported speech and ask students to identify which is which.

4 Report the statements below.
Students report statements using reported speech.
- Read aloud the first statement and elicit that it is an instance of direct speech (the words that someone actually said). Elicit the reported speech of the first item: *She asked how things were with Katie*. Then ask students to work alone or in pairs completing the rest of the activity. Check answers.

Answers
1. She asked how things were with Katie.
2. Emily told Jake to say Katie he liked her.
3. Jake said she had no feelings for him. 4. Emily said she would tell her how he felt if he didn't.

5 🎧²⁷ Now listen to Jake talking to Katie after school. Report two things they each said.
Students listen and report what a person said.
- Ask students to listen to the conversation once straight through for the main idea, then have students listen again and, working in pairs, report two things that were said. If students need help, write an example on the board. (*Jake said there was something he needed to tell her.*) Check and discuss answers.

Answers
Answers will vary.

Audio Script
KATIE: I'm so glad you're going with me, Jake! Thanks!
JAKE: I'm glad, too… Listen, Katie. There's something I need to tell you…
KATIE: Yeah?
JAKE: But I don't know how to say it…
KATIE: Jake, you're my best friend! You can tell me anything!
JAKE: OK. The thing is… it's very difficult for me to say, but…
KATIE: Come on, Jake! Spit it out!
JAKE: I… I hope you are very happy in Paris. I'm sure you're going to love studying French in Paris this summer.
KATIE: Is that what you wanted to tell me? Well, thanks… but I'm going to Aix-En-Provence, not Paris, you know…
JAKE: Oh! Ok…
KATIE: Now which bus should we take downtown?

6 Think Fast! Work with a partner. Report an imaginary conversation between Jake and Katie in which he really tells her how he feels.
Students do a one-minute timed challenge: reporting an imaginary conversation.
- Review the conversations featured on these two pages and elicit or clarify the fact that Jake likes Katie but has not told her about his feelings.
- Organize students into pairs and have them imagine a conversation in which Jake tells Katie how he feels. Then have students report the conversation. For example, Jake could report what happened to Emily.

> **Extension**
> Students look for real-life examples of reporting.
> - Ask students to search in print or online news sources for examples of reported speech about current topics in the news. Have students share their reports with the rest of the class.

Wrap-up
Students improvise a reported conversation.
- Organize students into pairs and invite them to improvise a conversation in which one of the speakers reports what was said in a previous conversation with another person. Encourage students to try various combinations of characters.

▶ **Workbook p. 152, Activities 3 and 4**

 **Reading & Writing**

Objectives
Students will be able to **identify text types**, **read for specific information**, and write an information leaflet.

Lesson 5   Student's Book pp. 102 and 103

> ✔ **Homework Check!**
> Workbook p. 152, Activities 3 and 4
>
> **Answers**
> **3 Read and circle the correct option in the sentence.**
> 1. to listen, 2. was doing, 3. had filled out, 4. was, 5. had gotten
> **4 Look and rewrite the sentences in reported speech.**
> 1. He asked if I had heard the news. 2. She said she was going to buy her plane ticket. 3. He told us to open our books. 4. She said her name was Vanessa. 5. They said they were ready to travel.

Warm-up
Students report recent conversations.
- Organize students into small groups and ask them to take turns reporting imaginary conversations that they had recently with celebrities, sports stars, politicians, etc. Encourage them to be imaginative.

 104

1 Look at the text and pictures. Underline the option that describes what kind of text it is.
Students identify text type.
- Ask students to look quickly at the text. Then have them select the correct description of the text type. Check the answer and ask students to say which specific items in the text helped them arrive at the answer.

Answer
2

2 Read the leaflet. Mark (✓) YES, NO or NOT MENTIONED for the statements below.
Students read for specific information.
- Read aloud the first statement and ask students to say if it is true (Y) or not (N), or whether it is not mentioned (NM), then have students work alone or in pairs completing the rest of the activity. Check answers.

Answer
1. Y, 2. NM, 3. NM, 4. N, 5. Y, 6. N, 7. N, 8. N

3 Think Fast! How many different countries are mentioned in the leaflet?
Students do a thirty-second timed challenge: finding all the countries mentioned in a text.
- Organize students into pairs and challenge them, in 30 seconds, to find and list all the countries mentioned in the text. Check answers.

Answer
15

Wrap-up
Students share ideas about destinations for study abroad.
- Organize students into small groups. In thirty seconds, each student has to say where in the world they would most like to go to study for a semester and why. Invite some students to share their ideas with the rest of the class.

➡ **Workbook p. 153, Activities 1 and 2**

> 🐝 **Teaching Tip**
> **Influencing the Learning Environment**
> You cannot control the architecture or the facilities of your classroom, but you do have some control over how your room looks. Working with your students, make the classroom a pleasant place to be, with an atmosphere that is conducive to learning.

Lesson 6   Student's Book p. 103

> ✔ **Homework Check!**
> Workbook p. 153, Activities 1 and 2
> **Answers**
> **1 Read the text and complete the headings of each body paragraph with the phrases below.**
> *top to bottom* makes you grow personally, opens your mind, gives you more career opportunities, helps you make life-long friends
> **2 Answer the questions in your notebook. Then discuss with a partner.**
> Answers will vary.

Warm-up
Students compare fonts, layout and design in a selection of published materials.
- Bring to class a selection of various magazines, newspapers, brochures, etc. and invite students to compare and contrast the materials referring to the fonts used, the layout of the text, the design, etc.

4 Look at the leaflet again. Read the sentences below and write T (True) or F (False).
Students identify aspects of layout and language in a text.
- Ask students to look again at the leaflet on page 102. Then have them look at the list of characteristics and features. Make sure that students know what fonts and bullet points are. Read aloud the first item and ask students to say if the leaflet exhibits this feature (*T*), then have students work alone or in pairs completing the rest of the activity. Check and discuss answers.

Answers
1. T, 2. F, 3. T, 4. T, 5. T, 6. T

Draw students' attention to the **Be Strategic!** box and ask them to read the information. Stress the importance of anticipating who the audience for a particular piece of writing might be, since this may well affect the writer's decisions regarding the content and layout of a text.

5 Work with a partner. Create a leaflet for a fictitious study program. Follow the steps below.
Students design and write leaflets for study programs abroad.
- Ask students to read through all the steps carefully. Deal with any queries that students may have. Then organize them into pairs and have them create their leaflets, giving sufficient attention to the type of study program, the audience, the use of persuasive language and the use of images and effective layout.

Answers
Answers will vary.

Stop and Think! Critical Thinking
Read your classmates' leaflets. Which of the study programs advertised would you like to attend? Why?
- Organize students into small groups and have them discuss which of their classmates' study programs they would like to attend.
- Invite groups to share their comments with the rest of the class.

> **Extension**
> Students share examples of persuasive writing in leaflets, brochures, etc.
> - Organize students into pairs and invite them to find examples of persuasive language as used in brochures, advertisements, etc. (in print or online) for educational products, courses, services, etc.

Wrap-up
Students devise sentences using items from the Glossary.
- Organize students into teams and challenge them, working within a time limit, to write one sentence for each of the items in the Glossary on page 103.

➡ **Workbook p. 153, Activity 3**

Preparing for the Next Lesson
Ask students to watch a short introduction to Ireland: goo.gl/uC57al or invite them to consult the following website: goo.gl/JATfvh

Objectives
Students will be able to understand and discuss some of Ireland's visitor attractions.

Lesson 7   Student's Book pp. 104 and 105

> ✔ **Homework Check!**
> Workbook p. 153, Activity 3
> **Answers**
> **3 In your notebook, write a reflection on what studying abroad would mean to you.**
> Answers will vary.

Warm-up
Students activate knowledge about Ireland.
- As a whole-class, quiz students on their knowledge of Ireland. Ask about, for example, its location (north western Europe), its Irish name (Éire), its capital city (Dublin), its population (approx. 4.75 million), its currency (the Euro / €).

1 Look at the pictures in the magazine. Match them to the captions.
Students match captions and photos in a magazine article.
- Elicit observation about what students can see in the photos. Have students work alone matching each caption with the correct photo. Check answers.

Answers
top to bottom, left to right 4, 2, 3, 1, 5

2 **Listen to an education agent talking with two students about studying in Ireland. Mark (✓) the advantages of studying in the country.**
Students listen for key ideas.
- Ask students to read the list of statements. Have them listen to the conversation and mark the advantages that they hear. Check answers.

Answers
2, 4, 5, 7

Audio Script
EDUCATION AGENT: I know that you are planning to do a full academic semester at a university in the United Kingdom, but have you ever considered going to Ireland?
FEMALE STUDENT: Ireland? Not really… is it a good study destination?
EDUCATION AGENT: It sure is! In Ireland, you can study at universities, specialist colleges or institutes of technology. Besides, tuition fees and cost of living are much lower in Dublin than in any major British city. In a nutshell, you would spend much less money to study in Ireland than in the UK.
MALE STUDENT: What is a specialist college?
EDUCATION AGENT: It's an institution that offers courses in a single subject area.
FEMALE STUDENT: Wow! I didn't know about that. But what about the educational level?
EDUCATION AGENT: Several higher ed institutions in Ireland rank extremely well internationally.
MALE STUDENT: Hmm… Tell us more about it!
EDUCATION AGENT: Trinity College, for example, is the oldest higher education institution in the country. It ranked 78th in the world! There are around 17,000 students enrolled in their courses. And its historical buildings are simply amazing! Take a look at this brochure…
FEMALE STUDENT: It really sounds interesting. But you know that besides studying, we also want to learn about another culture and travel a bit on weekends…
EDUCATION AGENT: You can definitely do that in Ireland! The country's culture is truly unique. There are several historic cities to visit and places of incredible natural beauty both in the countryside and on the coast. For example, you can visit castles in Cork or attend the Arts Festival in Galway.
MALE STUDENT: Wow, Vicky… Look at these cliffs on the coast!
FEMALE STUDENT: They look wonderful, Ben…

Wrap-up
Students compare Ireland with their own country.
- Set a time limit and ask students to brainstorm ways in which the landscape and attractions of Ireland are similar to those in their country and how they are different.

▶ **(No homework today.)**

> **Teaching Tip**
> **Developing Cultural Awareness**
> A person's cultural background often affects the way they interact in the classroom and how they learn English. Be aware also that differences can exist within cultures.

Lesson 12   Student's Book p. 109

Warm-up
Students leave messages about their experiences studying abroad.
- Ask students to imagine that they have just begun a period of study in a foreign country. Ask them to write a short summary of their impressions and reactions to the first few days of their stay. Invite students to share their work with the rest of the class.

4 Complete the reported statements with the correct verb form, changing the tense.
Students complete reported statements.
- Read aloud the first item of direct speech and elicit the correct way to convert it into reported speech (changing the verb from present to past). Then have students work alone or in pairs completing the rest of the activity, using the correct verb form and changing the tense as necessary.
- Check answers by having students read aloud the direct speech statement or question and then the reported speech version.

Answers

1. was so, 2. was studying, 3. there were, 4. was going, 5. had told, 6. would stay / decided

5 Collect direct quotes from the people below. Then report them.
Students gather examples of direct speech and then report them.
- Ask students to work alone writing examples of things that people said and then changing them into reported speech. Have students work in pairs checking each other's work.

Answers
Answers will vary.

Big Question
Students are given the opportunity to revisit the Big Question and reflect on it.
- Ask students to turn to the unit opener on page 97 and to look at the collage of pictures. Elicit observation and comment about what the images represent (friends, sightseeing, study, food, culture, etc.)
- Read aloud the question. Discuss the things that a person needs if they want to spend some time living and studying abroad. Focus not just on practical matters such as visas, tickets, accommodation, etc. or on material objects like books and clothes, but also on the character traits that a person needs to possess in order to make a success of a stay in another country, for example, patience, adaptability, openness, etc.

Scorecard
Hand out (and/or project) a *Scorecard*. Have students fill in their *Scorecards* for this unit.

➡ **Study for the unit test.**

8 What will I do in the future?

Grammar	Vocabulary
Future Continuous: <u>I'll be studying</u> photography at the Arts University. In ten years, <u>you will be running</u> the kitchen of your own restaurant!	**Future Goals:** academic life, action plan, deadlines, gap year, goals, graduate, graduation, healthier lifestyle, personal life, physical activities, professional life, resources, vocational school

Listening	Speaking
Listening and inferring	Giving a presentation

What will I do in the future?

In the first lesson, read the unit title aloud and have students look carefully at the unit cover. Encourage them to think about the message in the picture. At the end of the unit, students will discuss the big question: *What will I do in the future?*

Teaching Tip
Develop Yourself Professionally
Learning about new techniques, methods, and approaches helps you to keep up-to-date with changes in your field and it stops you from stagnating. Applying new techniques, methods, and approaches helps you plan and deliver interesting and effective lessons. Also, professional development can help you advance in your career. There are a number of ways you can develop yourself professionally. Continue your education. Join professional organizations and have access to a network of professionals. Keep up with current literature by reading English language teaching academic journals, magazines, newspapers and books.

Vocabulary

Objective
Students will be able to use **appropriate vocabulary** to talk about personal goals for the future.

Lesson 1   Student's Book pp. 112 and 113

Warm-up
Students recall childhood memories about occupations.
- Organize students into small groups and invite them to share memories of the jobs they thought they wanted to do when they were much younger. Open up the discussion for the whole class and elicit observations and comments.

1 Read the text on the computer screen. What is Mackenzie doing?
Students skim a text for the general idea.
- Ask students to look briefly at the text. Read the question aloud and elicit possible answers. Discuss with students the reasons why a person aged 17 might decide to make an action plan.

Answers

Answers will vary.

2 Add words from the text to complete the collocations in the chart. Not all of them will be completed now.
Students start to complete a chart with collocations.
- Ask students to look at the chart. Elicit a collocation from Mackenzie's text for the first verb, *have* (*have a healthier lifestyle*), then have students work alone or in pairs completing what they can of the chart with collocations from the text. Check answers.

Answers

1. have a healthier lifestyle, 2. be more sympathetic to others, 3. go to college,
4. get a job … , 5. start my own business … ,
6. rent an apartment … , 7. save money …

3 Add the phrases from the box to the chart in Activity 2 to form new collocations.
Students complete a chart with more collocations.
- Ask students to look at the collocations in the box. Have them work alone or in pairs adding these words and phrases to the chart, using appropriate collocations. Check answers.

Answers

1. have a less stressful routine, 2. be patient with my little sister, 3. go to vocational school, 4. get married, 5. start doing physical activities, 6. rent (an apartment [not included]), 7. save resources, like water, 8. take a gap year, 9. travel around the world, 10. buy a car

Wrap-up
Students brainstorm ideas for their own action plans.
- Organize students into pairs and ask them to brainstorm ideas for their own action plans, using Mackenzie's text as an example. Then invite them to share their ideas with the rest of the class.

▶ **Workbook p. 154, Activities 1 and 2**

 Teaching Tip
Working Out Vocabulary from Context
Encourage students to try to understand new vocabulary by guessing the meaning from the context in which it is used. By working out the meaning from the context, students are more likely to remember the word or phrase.

Lesson 2 Student's Book p. 113

✔ **Homework Check!**

Workbook p. 154, Activities 1 and 2

Answers

1 Complete the collocations. Then match them to the photos.
1. a car, 2. money, 3. around the world, 4. an apartment, 5. a healthier lifestyle
left-hand column, top to bottom save money (2), travel around the world (3), buy a car (1)
right-hand column, top to bottom get married (0), have a healthier lifestyle (5), rent an apartment (4)

2 Categorize the collocations from Activity 1 in the chart below.
Personal Development travel around the world, get married, have a healthier lifestyle
Financial Security save money, buy a car, rent an apartment

Warm-up
Students review the spelling of key vocabulary items.
- Carry out a quick spelling test of words related to personal action plans: *accommodation, academic, apartment, business, college, graduation, healthier, professional, resources, sympathetic*, etc.

4 Complete the statements and questions.
Students complete statements and questions with appropriate collocations.
- Ask students to look at the first item. Elicit a verb that collocates correctly with the noun phrase that follows (*take*). Then have students work alone or in pairs completing the rest of the statements and questions with collocations from Activities 2 and 3. Check answers.

Answers

1. take, 2. go, 3. have, 4. be, 5. start, 6. rent, 7. get, 8. buy / buy (get), 9. get, 10. start

5 Work in small groups. Choose four questions from Activity 4. Share your answers.
Students discuss their answers to questions in Activity 4.
- Organize students into small groups and have them select four questions from the previous activity. Ask them to think of their own answers before sharing and comparing them with their classmates. Then open up the discussion for the whole class.
- Draw students' attention to the **Guess What!** box. Read the information aloud and elicit observation and comment. Ask students if they think they would like to make an action plan.

Stop and Think! Critical Thinking
Do you think writing an action plan is a good idea? Why (not)?
- Organize students into small groups and have them discuss whether they think it is a good idea to write an action plan. Encourage them to come up with reasons either for or against.
- Invite groups to share their comments with the rest of the class.

> **Extension**
> Students find information about plans / ambitions of family members and friends when they were younger.
> - Ask students to ask adult family members and friends about the occupations they wanted to do when they were younger. Invite students to share information with the rest of the class.

Wrap-up
Students make lists of collocations.
- Organize students into teams and challenge them, against the clock, to come up with two lists: a list of more noun collocations, as in Activities 2 and 3 (e.g., *travel around the world*), and a list of more verb collocations (e.g., *attend vocational school*)

➡ **Workbook pp. 154 and 155, Activities 3 and 4**

Grammar

Objectives
Students will be able to use the **future continuous** to describe actions at a particular moment in the future.

Lesson 3 Student's Book pp. 114 and 115

> ✔ **Homework Check!**
> Workbook pp. 154 and 155, Activities 3 and 4
> **Answers**
> **3 Complete the sentences with the collocations below.**
> 1. start my own business, 2. take a gap year, 3. go to vocational school, 4. get a job, 5. save resources
> **4 Complete the collocations with the correct form of the verb and match each question to its answer.**
> 1. saving, 2. have, 3. travel, 4. saving, 5. start,
> 1. f, 2. a, 3. b, 4. c, 5. e

Warm-up
Students speculate about jobs in the future.
- Organize students into small groups and invite them to make a list of at least five jobs that do not exist at the moment but that may well exist ten or fifteen years from now.

1 Read the conversation. What is Mackenzie writing about?
Students skim a conversation for the general idea.
- Ask students to work alone skimming quickly through the conversation. Ask them to find what Mackenzie is writing about. Check the answer.

Answers
She is writing her action plan with future goals, specifically for ten years from now.

- Draw students' attention to the box with information about the *Future continuous* and clarify any doubts that students may have about form or meaning.

2 Circle examples of the future continuous in Activity 1.
Students identify instances of the future continuous in a conversation.
- Ask students to look at the conversation on the opposite page. Have them circle examples of the future continuous. Check answers.

Answers
I'll be working, I'll be living, I'll be studying, I won't be working, you will be running, I'll be visiting

Stop and Think! Critical Thinking
Who is more likely to reach their goals, Mackenzie or Cameron? Why?
- Organize students into small groups and have them discuss who they think is most likely to achieve their goals, Mackenzie or Cameron, and why.
- Invite groups to share their comments with the rest of the class.

Wrap-up
Students role-play conversations about their personal action plans for the future.
- Organize students into pairs and invite them to role-play conversations about their action plans for the future. Invite pairs of students to share their conversations with the rest of the class.

➡ **Workbook p. 155, Activities 1 and 2**

 **Teaching Tip**
Making Good Use of Teacher Talk
Teacher talk in class is an excellent source of comprehensible input. Of course, you want your students to be active language users for much of the lesson, but you also want to give them opportunities to hear a lot of comprehensible English and to learn from it. The best opportunities for this come from your own speech, which is probably better than recordings or movies because it is directly addressed to your students and it is taking place in real time.

Lesson 4   Student's Book p. 115

> ✔ **Homework Check!**
> Workbook p. 155, Activities 1 and 2
> **Answers**
> **1 Write sentences in the future continuous.**
> 1. What will your sister be studying at college next year? She'll be studying law. 2. What classes will you be taking next semester? I'll be taking social science and economics. 3. Where will you be living in a couple of years? I'll be living in the US. 4. Who will be waiting for you at the airport? George will be waiting for me.
> **2 Complete the sentences with the correct form of future continuous.**
> 1. will be waiting, 2. won't be coming, 3. will be taking, 4. will be working, 5. won't be studying

Warm-up
Students review the spelling rules for the continuous forms of verbs.
- Check students' knowledge of the spelling rules for the continuous forms of verbs with a quick dictation test, for example, *play-playing, begin-beginning, lie-lying, dance-dancing.*

3 Read a letter another student wrote to her "future self". Fill in the gaps with the future continuous forms of the verbs in parentheses.
Students complete a text with future continuous forms.
- Ask students to look briefly at the letter. Make sure that they understand the basic concept of writing to one's future self. Have them complete the letter with the correct future continuous forms of the given verbs. Check answers.

Answers
1. will be working, 2. will be treating, 3. will be taking care, 4. will be living, 5. will be seeing, 6. will be enjoying, 7. will be traveling, 8. will / be spending, 9. will / be laughing

4 Write sentences in the future continuous to express the plans below. Use the prompts.
Students write future continuous sentences from prompts.
- Read aloud the first item and the prompt. Elicit the correct future continuous sentence (*In three years' time, Kevin will be working as an engineer.*), then have students work alone or in pairs completing the rest of the activity. Check answers.

Answers
1. In three years' time, Kevin will be working as an engineer. 2. Next year, Savannah will be living and studying in Spain. 3. Next semester, our teacher won't be teaching our class anymore. 4. After summer, I won't be seeing my friend every day.

5 What are your plans? Write about yourself.
Students write about their own plans using the future continuous.
- Read aloud the first item and elicit a few suggestions. Have students work alone writing about their own plans, then ask students to share and compare their ideas in pairs. Elicit answers from the whole class.

Answers
Answers will vary.

> **Extension**
> Students make predictions about the lives of famous people.
> - Ask students to work in pairs compiling a list of predictions about what certain famous people (politicians, actors, athletes, etc.) will be doing ten years from now. Invite students to share their ideas with the rest of the class.

Wrap-up
Students play a guessing game about future plans.
- Organize students into small groups and invite them to play a guessing game. One player makes three statements about their future plans – one true statement and two false. The other players try to guess which is the genuine plan.

▶ **Workbook p. 156, Activities 3 and 4**

Stop and Think! Critical Thinking
Who is likely to reach their goals, Mackenzie or Cameron? Why?
- Refer students to Mackenzie and Cameron's situations and ask them to mention their goals, according to the conversation.
- Have students work in pairs and discuss who they think is more likely to reach their goals. Encourage students to justify their answers. Give students enough time to come to a conclusion.
- In order to present their ideas, pairs should take turns to talk about Mackenzie and Cameron.
- Give each pair five minutes to present their ideas. (Use your Stopwatch app to time the discussion.)

Listening & Speaking

Objectives
Students will be able to **listen and infer meaning**, and **give an oral presentation**.

Lesson 5 — Student's Book pp. 116 and 117

> ✔ **Homework Check!**
> Workbook p. 156, Activities 3 and 4
> Answers
> **3 Look at the time line and write activities Sandra will be doing in the future.**
> 1. She'll be going to college. 2. She'll be working.
> 3. She'll be living in New York.
> **4 Write about what you will be doing in the future.**
> Answers will vary.

Warm-up
Students react to a series of predictions.
- Using the future continuous, make a series of predictions about your school ten years from now. Ask students to say if they agree or disagree.

1 Look at the picture. What can you infer about the situation? Underline the correct answers.
Students make inferences about a picture.
- Ask students to look at the whole two-page picture. Have them answer the questions in pairs. Make clear that they have to infer, deduce something from partial evidence and reasoning, rather than from explicit statements. Check and discuss answers.

Answers
1. Person #3, 2. b

2 ²⁹ **Listen to Sean. Complete the statements below. Your inferences in Activity 1 will help you.**
Students listen for specific information.
- Ask students to listen to the audio and complete the statements. Check answers.

Answers
1. four, 2. universities / study 3. traditional, 4. area / study

Audio Script
SEAN: Good morning, guys.
Hi, Mr. Roberts.
As part of our tasks for Mr. Roberts' class, I'm going to talk about career paths in Computer Science today. Let me outline the structure of my presentation. First, I'll give you some basic information about Computer Science. Secondly, I'll talk about universities and colleges that offer this major in and out of our state. Next, I'll discuss the different areas a person who graduates in Computer Science can work at. Last of all, I'll open to your questions, so I ask you to leave questions to the end of my presentation.
So let's start by defining what Computer Science is. Computer science, also known as CS, is basically the study of computers and of their systems. It involves mainly working with designing, developing and applying software programs. Knowing how to program is vital for any computer scientist, but it's far from being the only area of study in this major. There are other traditional fields, such as computer security, networks and systems, database analysis and software engineering. And there are also new, promising and exciting areas of study emerging, such as Artificial Intelligence, human-computer interaction and bioinformatics.
STUDENT: Can I ask a question?
SEAN: Yes, of course!
STUDENT: How about computer language programming? You didn't mention that...
SEAN: Well, this area was mentioned at the beginning of this section of my presentation, actually. As I said, computer programming is a very important area of study in CS. It's here on my slide, as you can see.
Now, moving on... Considering the places where one can study, there are several institutions that offer CS as a major in our state and also in neighboring states...

Wrap-up
Students play How Many Words?
- Write on the board a word or phrase from the audio (for example, *bioinformatics, computer science*). Challenge students to see how many words they can make using just letters from the word or phrase. (*form / sit / in / put / mop / niece*)

▶ **Workbook p. 157, Activities 1 and 2**

> 💬 **Teaching Tip**
> **Using L1 in Class**
> Occasional use of L1 in class can add clarity, provide useful insights into how language works, and save time that can then be used for further engagement with English.

Lesson 6 Student's Book p. 117

> ✔ **Homework Check!**
> Workbook p. 157, Activities 1 and 2
> **Answers**
> **1 Answer the following questions *T* (True) or *F* (False) about your savings habits.**
> Answers will vary.
> **2 Answer the following questions in your notebook. Then share your answers with a partner.**
> 1. Exponential growth is growth that gets quicker in proportion to the growing total size. 2. $1,100, $1,210, 3. Answers will vary.

Warm-up
Students share their experiences of giving presentations.
- In small groups, have students discuss their experiences with oral presentations.

3 🎧²⁹ **Listen to Sean again. What can you infer about him, his presentation and one of his classmates? Circle *T* (true) or *F* (false).**
Students listen and infer information.
- Ask students to read through the questions. Then have them listen again to the audio and mark the statements as true or false. Check and discuss answers. Talk about the clues that students found that helped them arrive at their answers.
- Draw students' attention to the **Be Strategic!** box and ask them to read the information. Stress the importance of using clues within a text and also one's existing knowledge of how people usually behave in certain situations.

Answers
1. F, 2. T, 3. T, 4. Answer will vary. 5. T

4 Look at some signposting language used in presentations. Organize the items in the chart.
Students design and write leaflets for study programs abroad.
- Ask students to read through all the items and to organize them into categories in the chart. Check answers.

Answers
Greeting Your Audience: d, e, Outlining the Presentation: i, j, n, Starting a Topic: c, k, Referring to Your Visuals: a, l, m, Inviting Questions: b, g, Ending Your Presentation and Thanking the Audience: f, h, o, p

5 Now prepare a presentation on a college major. Follow the steps below.
- Ask students to read through all the steps carefully. Then have them work alone or in pairs on their presentation about a college major of their choice.

Answers
Answers will vary.

6 Give your presentation to the class. What important things did you learn from your classmates' information?
- Invite pairs of students to give their presentations. Encourage students to take notes as they listen and to ask questions at the end.

Answers
Answers will vary.

7 Think Fast! As a class, list all the majors mentioned in your presentations!
Students do a 45-second timed challenge: listing all the college majors mentioned in their presentations.
- Set the time limit and have students work together listing as many college majors as they can. Check answers.

Answers
Answers will vary.

> **Extension**
> Students research the top ten most popular majors in the US and in their own country.
> - Organize students into small groups and ask them to look for information about the most popular college majors. Have them present their findings to the class.

Wrap-up
Students list more examples of signposting language.
- Organize students into pairs and, working to a time limit, challenge them to come up with at least one more example of signposting language for each of the categories in Activity 4.

➡ **Workbook p. 157, Activity 3**

Preparing for the Next Lesson
Ask students to watch a short introduction to Norway: goo.gl/CPzuBf or invite them to consult the following website: goo.gl/oCc5r3

Culture

Objectives
Students will be able to understand and discuss the advantages that Norway offers to young people.

Lesson 7   Student's Book p. 118

> ✔ **Homework Check!**
> Workbook p. 157, Activity 3
> **Answers**
> 3 Create a savings action plan in your notebook.
> Answers will vary.

Warm-up
Students share and compare impressions of Norway.
- Organize students into small groups and have them share and compare their impressions of Norway. To elicit initial ideas, ask, for example, *What do you think the climate is like? Do you think it has a large population? What does the landscape look like?*

1 What do you know about Norway? Complete the fact file with information from the box. Then search online to check your answers.
Students complete a fact file with information about Norway.
- Ask students to look at the background photo. Elicit that it shows the Norwegian flag. Ask what time of year they think the photo was taken. Then ask students to look at the fact file at the foot of the page. Organize students into small groups and have them try to complete the chart without help. Ask students to check their answers online. Check and discuss answers.

Answers
Capital city: Oslo, Population: approx. 5 million, Percentage of the population 15–24 years old: 13.1%, GDP (per capita / year): US$69,712, Interesting fact: a few

> **Extension**
> Students research a well-known person from Norway.
> - Organize students into small groups and ask them to look for information about a famous person from Norway. Have them give a presentation to the class about their chosen figure and their achievements.

Wrap-up
Students compare Norway with their own country.
- Set a time limit and ask students to brainstorm ways in which Norway is similar to their country and how it is different.
- Elicit students' reactions to the information presented on page 118.

➡ **(No homework today.)**

 Teaching Tip
Using Songs in Class
Songs are an enjoyable way for students to learn English since they provide an authentic source of English language usage. Songs are useful for listening, reading, and pronunciation skills. Generally speaking, slow songs are useful for improving listening skills. Songs with longer lyrics can be used for practicing reading. Songs with repetitive lyrics can be used to concentrate on specific pronunciation items and language structures.

Lesson 8   Student's Book p. 119

Warm-up
Students recap information about Norway.
- With books closed, conduct a quick-fire quiz to recap facts about Norway.

2 Read the article and answer the questions.
Students read an article and answer comprehension questions.
- Ask students to read through all the questions. Have students work alone or in pairs answering the questions by referring to the article on page 118. Check answers. In each case, ask students to show where in the text they found the answer.

Answers
1. 15-24 years. 2. 64 countries. 3. Available to young Norwegians. 4. A positive environment. 5. No, they are not discriminated. 6. Long … they last around 20 hours.

3 Discuss the answers as a class.
Students discuss their answers to the questions in Activity 2.
- Organize students into small groups and have them compare and discuss their answers to the questions in the previous activity.

Stop and Think! Critical Thinking
Considering the four criteria included in the article, would your country rank high or low in the Youthonomics Global Index? Why?
- Organize students into small groups and have them discuss how high or how low they think their country would rank in the Youthonomics Global Index? Encourage them to give reasons for their answers.
- Invite groups to share their ideas with the rest of the class.

> **Extension**
> Students research Norway's facts and figures.
> - Organize students into small groups and ask them to prepare a presentation about only one of the items in the Glossary on page 119 (*vocational training, entrepreneur, civil rights*).
> - Have students share their presentations with the rest of the class.

Wrap-up
Students role-play conversations about opportunities for young people in Norway.
- Organize students into pairs and have them role-play conversations in which a young Norwegian person tells a visitor from abroad about the attractive living conditions of young people in Norway – education, vocational training, employment, working conditions, well-being, etc.

(No homework today.)

> **Teaching Tip**
> **Managing Fast Finishers**
> Some students complete activities more quickly than others, so it's a good idea to have a few extra activities on hand, otherwise these students may become bored and disruptive. One set of activities designed for fast finishers are the **Just for Fun** pages. Students can work on these individually and then check their answers in the back of the Student's Book. The *Just for Fun* activities for this unit are on page 124.

 **Project**

Objectives
Students will be able to create an action plan for something they want to achieve.

Lesson 9   Student's Book pp. 120 and 121

Warm-up
Students devise self-quiz questions to determine how good people are at planning.
- Organize students into small groups and have them come up with two or three self-quiz questions that can help a person find out how good they are at planning for the future. Questions could ask about people's tendency to make plans contrasted with a tendency to improvise, for example.

1 Read the action plan for Connor's future academic life. Choose a heading from the box for each column.
Students match column headings with sections in a chart.
- Ask students to look at the chart. Elicit that it shows a person's action plan for academic aspects of their life. Have students work alone or in pairs matching each of the headings with the correct column in the chart. Check and discuss answers.

Answers
from left to right Tasks, Action, Deadline, Resources (People / Things), Problem and Possible Solution

- Draw students' attention to the *Guess What!* box. Read the information aloud and elicit observation and comment. Ask students what they know about the academic requirements for students wanting to enroll in a medical school. Elicit the names of institutions in their country where people can train to become doctors.

2 Work in small groups. Read the action plan again and discuss the questions below.
Students answer discussion questions in small groups.
- Ask students to read through all the questions. Then have them work in small groups discussing their answers to the questions. Check and discuss answers as a whole class.

Answers
Answers will vary.

Wrap-up
Students speculate about the future of Connor Nowak.
- Organize students into pairs and have them speculate and invent a future life for Connor Nowak. Ask them to use the future continuous to describe his future life, for example, *Four years from now, he will be finishing his pre-med course in biology.* Encourage students to use their imagination! Ask pairs of students to share their ideas with the rest of the class. Invite observation and comment about the various "lives" of Connor Nowak.

 (No homework today.)

> **Teaching Tip**
> **Eliciting Vocabulary from Other Students**
> When a student asks you about a certain vocabulary item, first ask other members of the class if they can help. Remember that, generally, different students know different words. So there is usually a high probability that somebody in the room has come across that vocabulary before.

Lesson 10 Student's Book p. 121

Warm-up
Students go over the spelling of vocabulary items, focusing on double letters.
- Carry out a quick spelling test of words from these pages that have double letters: *appointment, carefully, difficult, enroll, recommendations, suggestions, word processor.*

3 Write an action plan for something you want to achieve in your life. Follow the steps below.
Students create an action plan.
- Ask students to read through all of the steps of the instructions. Encourage them to use the action plan on the previous page as a model, though they are free to adapt and improve it as they wish.
- Adopt a slightly different way of working for this project. Ask students to work alone on each step and then to consult with a partner at the end of each step to consult, exchange suggestions, etc. before moving on to the next part.

Answers
Answers will vary.

4 Work in small groups. Share your action plan with your classmates.
Students share their work with classmates.
- Organize students into small groups and have them share their work with their classmates and comment on it. Then invite students to share their action plans with the rest of the class.

Stop and Think! Critical Thinking
Do you think your action plan will help you reach your objective? If so, why?
- Organize students into small groups and have them discuss whether they think their action plan will help them reach your objective and, if so, how and why.
- Invite groups to share their ideas with the rest of the class.

The Digital Touch
To incorporate digital media in the project, suggest one or more of the following:
- Invite students to create their action plans using PowerPoint or a similar slide show presentation program.
- If possible, allow students to upload their work to the school's website.

Note that students should have the option to do a task on paper or digitally.

Wrap-up
Students write fictional future biographies for their classmates.
- Organize students into pairs and ask them to exchange action plans. In each pair, each student writes a fictional biography based on the steps and events in their partner's action plan. Invite students to share their future biographies with the rest of the class.

➡ **Workbook p. 156, Activity 1 (Review)**

Review

Objective
Students will be able to consolidate their understanding of the vocabulary and grammar learned in the unit.

Lesson 11   Student's Book p. 122

✔ **Homework Check!**
Workbook p. 156, Activity 1 (Review)

Answers
1 Complete each sentence describing what Brad will be doing after he graduates from college.
1. … he will be saving his money. 2. … he will be starting his own company. 3. … he will be getting married. 4. … he will be buying a new car. 5. … he will be buying a house.

Warm-up
Students revise irregular verb forms.
- Carry out a quick-fire oral test of students' knowledge of irregular verbs in their base form, their past simple form, and their past participle form. For example, say *buy* to elicit *buy-bought-bought*.

1 Underline the correct word to complete the collocations.
Students select the correct collocation in a series of phrases.
- Read aloud the first phrase and elicit the correct answer (*be*), then have students work alone or in pairs to complete the rest of the exercise. Check answers.

Answers
1. be, 2. buy, 3. get, 4. get, 5. have, 6. rent, 7. save, 8. save, 9. start, 10. take, 11. travel

2 Use the collocations from Activity 1 to label the pictures.
Students label photos with verb-noun collocations from the previous activity.
- Ask students to look at the first picture. Elicit the correct phrase (*start doing physical exercise*) and then have students work alone or in pairs completing the rest of the exercise. Check answers.

Answers
1. start doing physical exercise, 2. get a job, 3. travel around the world, 4. save money to buy a house, 5. buy a car, 6. get married

3 Are the sentences right (✓) or wrong (✗)? Look at the underlined information and rewrite the incorrect ones.
Students mark sentences as correct or incorrect in their use of collocations and then correct them.
- Ask students to work alone or in pairs marking the sentences as correct or incorrect as regards their use of collocations (the underlined phrases). Have them rewrite the incorrect sentences with the correct collocations. Check answers by having students read the corrected sentences aloud.

Answers
1. ✗ be more patient, 2. ✓, 3. ✓, 4. ✗ rent an apartment

Wrap-up
Students devise role plays based on given situations.
- Organize students into pairs and have them come up with role plays that use the statements or questions in Activity 3 as a starting point.

 (No homework today.)

🐝 Teaching Tip

Cooperating with Other Teachers
All teachers have experience and each teacher's experience is unique. Look for various ways to share what you have learned and to exchange ideas, tips, advice, and encouragement with colleagues. This can be in person or via various online forums.

Lesson 12   Student's Book p. 123

Warm-up

Students identify present, past, and future continuous sentences.

- Write on the board a selection of continuous sentence forms – some present, some past, and some future. Have students identify the form of each sentence.

4 Unscramble the sentences.

Students unscramble future continuous questions.

- Ask students to work alone or in pairs unscrambling the future continuous questions. Check answers by having students read the unscrambled questions aloud.

Answers

1. Will Lucy be working after the holiday? 2. Will you be studying English on Thursday afternoon? 3. Will Mike and Dave be traveling to the United States this summer? 4. Will Fred Dawson be training to be a doctor at this time next year?

5 Match the questions in Activity 4 to the pictures. Then answer.

Students match future continuous questions with pictures and answer the questions.

- Ask students to work alone or in pairs matching each question from the previous activity with the correct picture. Then have them answer the questions according to the information in the pictures. Check answers by having pairs of students read the questions and the answers aloud.

Answers

top row, left to right 2 Yes, I will., 4 Yes, he will.
bottom row, left to right 3 No, they won't. They'll be traveling to Italy., 1 No, she won't. She'll be taking the day off.

6 Complete the sentences with the correct form of the future continuous.

Students complete sentences with the correct future continuous form.

- Ask students to work alone or in pairs completing each sentence with the correct future continuous form of the given verb. Check answers.

Answers

1. will be learning, 2. will be getting, 3. Will / be studying, 4. will be taking, 5. will be living, 6. will / be doing

7 Answer the questions. Share your answers with a partner.

- Ask students to work alone answering the questions with information that is true for them. Then have students share and check their work. Invite students to share their answers with the class.

Answers

Answers will vary.

❓ Big Question

Students are given the opportunity to revisit the Big Question and reflect on it.

- Ask students to turn to the unit opener on page 111 and to look at the picture. Elicit observation and comment about what the image represents (a young person's thoughts about their future career choices).
- Read aloud the question. Discuss how a young person may feel excited about future career opportunities while at the same time feeling confused or overwhelmed by enormous amounts of information. Talk about how this is perfectly normal and that a lot of young people experience mixed emotions regarding the world of work. Elicit ideas about the people who students can turn to for help with career guidance.

⭐ Scorecard

Hand out (and / or project) a *Scorecard*. Have students fill in their *Scorecards* for this unit.

▶ **Study for the unit test.**

CD1 and CD2 Contents

CD 1

Worksheets

- **Grammar Worksheets**
  - Stopwatch 6 Answer Key Grammar.pdf
  - Stopwatch 6 Unit 0 Grammar 1 (6.0.G1).pdf
  - Stopwatch 6 Unit 0 Grammar 2 (6.0.G2).pdf
  - Stopwatch 6 Unit 1 Grammar 1 (6.1.G1).pdf
  - Stopwatch 6 Unit 1 Grammar 2 (6.1.G2).pdf
  - Stopwatch 6 Unit 2 Grammar 1 (6.2.G1).pdf
  - Stopwatch 6 Unit 2 Grammar 2 (6.2.G2).pdf
  - Stopwatch 6 Unit 3 Grammar 1 (6.3.G1).pdf
  - Stopwatch 6 Unit 3 Grammar 2 (6.3.G2).pdf
  - Stopwatch 6 Unit 4 Grammar 1 (6.4.G1).pdf
  - Stopwatch 6 Unit 4 Grammar 2 (6.4.G2).pdf
  - Stopwatch 6 Unit 5 Grammar 1 (6.5.G1).pdf
  - Stopwatch 6 Unit 5 Grammar 2 (6.5.G2).pdf
  - Stopwatch 6 Unit 6 Grammar 1 (6.6.G1).pdf
  - Stopwatch 6 Unit 6 Grammar 2 (6.6.G2).pdf
  - Stopwatch 6 Unit 7 Grammar 1 (6.7.G1).pdf
  - Stopwatch 6 Unit 7 Grammar 2 (6.7.G2).pdf
  - Stopwatch 6 Unit 8 Grammar 1 (6.8.G1).pdf
  - Stopwatch 6 Unit 8 Grammar 2 (6.8.G2).pdf

- **Reading Worksheets**
  - Stopwatch 6 Answer Key Reading.pdf
  - Stopwatch6 Unit 1 Reading 1 (6.1.R1).pdf
  - Stopwatch6 Unit 1 Reading 2 (6.1.R2).pdf
  - Stopwatch6 Unit 2 Reading 1 (6.2.R1).pdf
  - Stopwatch6 Unit 2 Reading 2 (6.2.R2).pdf
  - Stopwatch6 Unit 3 Reading 1 (6.3.R1).pdf
  - Stopwatch6 Unit 3 Reading 2 (6.3.R2).pdf
  - Stopwatch6 Unit 4 Reading 1 (6.4.R1).pdf
  - Stopwatch6 Unit 4 Reading 2 (6.4.R2).pdf
  - Stopwatch6 Unit 5 Reading 1 (6.5.R1).pdf
  - Stopwatch6 Unit 5 Reading 2 (6.5.R2).pdf
  - Stopwatch6 Unit 6 Reading 1 (6.6.R1).pdf
  - Stopwatch6 Unit 6 Reading 2 (6.6.R2).pdf
  - Stopwatch6 Unit 7 Reading 1 (6.7.R1).pdf
  - Stopwatch6 Unit 7 Reading 2 (6.7.R2).pdf
  - Stopwatch6 Unit 8 Reading 1 (6.8.R1).pdf
  - Stopwatch6 Unit 8 Reading 2 (6.8.R2).pdf

- **Vocabulary Worksheets**
  - Stopwatch 6 Unit 0 Vocabulary 1 (6.0.V1).pdf
  - Stopwatch 6 Unit 0 Vocabulary 1 (6.0.V2).pdf
  - Stopwatch 6 Unit 1 Vocabulary 1 (6.1.V1).pdf
  - Stopwatch 6 Unit 1 Vocabulary 2 (6.1.V2).pdf
  - Stopwatch 6 Unit 2 Vocabulary 1 (6.2.V1).pdf
  - Stopwatch 6 Unit 2 Vocabulary 2 (6.2.V2).pdf
  - Stopwatch 6 Unit 3 Vocabulary 1 (6.3.V1).pdf
  - Stopwatch 6 Unit 3 Vocabulary 2 (6.3.V2).pdf
  - Stopwatch 6 Unit 4 Vocabulary 1 (6.4.V1).pdf
  - Stopwatch 6 Unit 4 Vocabulary 2 (6.4.V2).pdf
  - Stopwatch 6 Unit 5 Vocabulary 1 (6.5.V1).pdf
  - Stopwatch 6 Unit 5 Vocabulary 2 (6.5.V2).pdf
  - Stopwatch 6 Unit 6 Vocabulary 1 (6.6.V1).pdf
  - Stopwatch 6 Unit 6 Vocabulary 2 (6.6.V2).pdf
  - Stopwatch 6 Unit 7 Vocabulary 1 (6.7.V1).pdf
  - Stopwatch 6 Unit 7 Vocabulary 2 (6.7.V2).pdf
  - Stopwatch 6 Unit 8 Vocabulary 1 (6.8.V1).pdf
  - Stopwatch 6 Unit 8 Vocabulary 2 (6.8.V2).pdf
  - Stopwatch 6 Vocabulary Answer Key.pdf

Class Audio CD 1
- Track 1—Track 29

CD 2

- **Project Rubrics**
  - Stopwatch 6 Project Rubrics.pdf
- **Scorecard** ★
  - Stopwatch 6 Scorecard.pdf
- **Test**
  - **Final Test**
    - Stopwatch 6 Answer Key Final Test.pdf
    - Stopwatch 6 Final Test.pdf
  - **Mid-Term Test**
    - Stopwatch 6 Answer Key Mid-Term Test.pdf
    - Stopwatch 6 Mid-Term.pdf
  - **Placement Test**
    - Stopwatch Placement Test Answer Key.pdf
    - Stopwatch Placement Test.pdf
  - **Standard Test**
    - Stopwatch 6 Answer Key Standard Test.pdf
    - Stopwatch 6 Standard Test U1.pdf
    - Stopwatch 6 Standard Test U2.pdf
    - Stopwatch 6 Standard Test U3.pdf
    - Stopwatch 6 Standard Test U4.pdf
    - Stopwatch 6 Standard Test U5.pdf
    - Stopwatch 6 Standard Test U6.pdf
    - Stopwatch 6 Standard Test U7.pdf
    - Stopwatch 6 Standard Test U8.pdf
  - **Test Plus**
    - Stopwatch 6 Answer Key Test Plus.pdf
    - Stopwatch 6 Test Plus U1.pdf
    - Stopwatch 6 Test Plus U2.pdf
    - Stopwatch 6 Test Plus U3.pdf
    - Stopwatch 6 Test Plus U4.pdf
    - Stopwatch 6 Test Plus U5.pdf
    - Stopwatch 6 Test Plus U6.pdf
    - Stopwatch 6 Test Plus U7.pdf
    - Stopwatch 6 Test Plus U8.pdf

Test Audio CD 2
- Track 1—Track 8 Unit Tests
- Track 9 Mid-Term
- Track 10 Final Test

Verb List

Base Form	Past	Past Participle	Base Form	Past	Past Participle
abduct	abducted	abducted	laugh	laughed	laughed
answer	answered	answered	learn	learned	learned
apply	applied	applied	like	liked	liked
arrest	arrested	arrested	live	lived	lived
ask	asked	asked	make	made	made
attend	attended	attended	manufacture	manufactured	manufactured
bake	baked	baked	meet	met	met
be	was / were	been	melt	melted	melted
become	became	become	miss	missed	missed
behave	behaved	behaved	play	played	played
break	broke	broke	produce	produced	produced
bring	brought	brought	record	recorded	recorded
build	built	built	rent	rented	rented
buy	bought	bought	ride	rode	ridden
care	cared	cared	rise	rose	risen
carry	carried	carried	run	ran	run
choose	chose	chosen	save	saved	saved
clean	cleaned	cleaned	say	said	said
crash	crashed	crashed	see	saw	seen
depict	depicted	depicted	sell	sold	sold
develop	developed	developed	send	sent	sent
die	died	died	show	showed	shown
do	did	done	sneak	sneaked	sneaked
draw	drew	drawn	spend	spent	spent
drop	dropped	dropped	study	studied	studied
eat	ate	eaten	take	took	taken
enjoy	enjoyed	enjoyed	tell	told	told
enroll	enrolled	enrolled	think	thought	thought
fall	fell	fallen	throw	threw	thrown
feed	fed	fed	tour	toured	toured
fight	fought	fought	travel	traveled	traveled
find	found	found	try	tried	tried
forget	forgot	forgotten	wake	woke	waken
found	founded	founded	win	won	won
get	got	gotten	work	worked	worked
give	gave	given	write	wrote	written
go	went	gone			
grow	grew	grown			
happen	happened	happened			
have	had	had			
help	helped	helped			
hire	hired	hired			
hit	hit	hit			
join	joined	joined			
keep	kept	kept			
know	knew	known